COAL MINES TO UC BERKELEY:

A DOOR TO DOOR SALESMAN'S JOURNEY

by John R. Horan

ALWAYS WAKE UP LAUGHING

ISBN 978-0-926664-44-9

Book and Cover Design: Chris Carlsson

COVER PHOTOS:
Coal miner by Lee Stone
Sather Gate at UC Berkeley by Tamara Evans

Printed in the United States

COAL MINES TO UC BERKELEY:
A DOOR TO DOOR SALESMAN'S JOURNEY

by John R. Horan

ALWAYS WAKE UP LAUGHING

1: DOOR TO DOOR FROM MIAMI TO SEATTLE, LA TO BOSTON

The Temple 7

The Bar Mitzvah Watch 8

Goodbye Shingle-town 11

The Hill 13

Flowers Don't Grow In The Coal Mines 15

Easy Times 16

Cathedral School 17

Boot Camp 19

Washing Dishes In The Pocono Mountains 21

Chasing Golf Balls At Skytop Lodge 25

Door To Door 28

Reader's Service Traveling Bookstore 31

Thumbing Back To Scranton 39

Crew Manager: Encyclopedia Road Show 42

On The Road Again 43

2: HITTING DOORS IN EUROPE 47

Herr Juegle Teaches Flying 50

Ziegfried Teaches Me English 51

Back To School: Like I Mean It 52

3: HITTING DOORS IN BERKELEY 55

Unloading Ships: The San Francisco Waterfront 59

Jack 60

Loading Box Cars 62

The Cannery 64

Cabbie...65

Dog Patch 67

Chinatown 67

The Chen Family 69

Pere Jacques Valente L'Ecole Polytechnique 69

Von Kneffel: Bracero 71

Boston 72

Bay of Pigs 72

Brave New World 73

Graduation 74

A Paycheck 76

1: DOOR TO DOOR FROM MIAMI TO SEATTLE, LA TO BOSTON

Approaching from the East, we see the car-cases of car wrecks covering the entire mountainside: Louis de Veronese's used car part inventory, the world's largest? Louis had made generous donations to the city including the WWII tank that adorned the traffic circle at the town's entrance.

Approaching from Carbondale to the North or from the West in the dark: we see below in the valley little blue flames of methane gas creeping over the hills of culm, the low energy coal waste mixture of rock and coal discards. We smell and breathe sulfur.

The sign on the traffic circle next to the WWII tank says:

"Welcome to Scranton, the Anthracite Coal Capital of the World."

THE TEMPLE

Leah Vercheck was opening the mail at the Temple Emmanuel in the once fashionable Hill section.

"Irving, here's a letter from a lawyer in Palo Alto, California. A Richie Horan left money to the Temple in honor of Keddy Shulowitz. You know the Shulowitz who owned the brewery? Had the mansion on Clay and Myrtle Streets. Horan? Doesn't sound Jewish."

"You don't have to be Jewish to give money away. Can I see it?"

"Central High, Class of 51. So born about 1934. He must have been about 80. I know someone who might know, Celine Fearson. A looker that one. She would have graduated in the early Fifties. She keeps the records for class re-unions. Ok I'll ask Celine: Horan Richie, right?"

THE BAR MITZVAH WATCH

"Richie look here." I turned to look and my shovel missed the furnace hopper door, the marble sized coal spilling on the floor. I grabbed the broom and started to sweep. As a short fourth grader with the hopper doors above my shoulders I had to slide the coal through the air just right otherwise sweep up the spilled coal.

"Just leave it." He held out a shiny gold pocket watch. "It's for you."

Dad—only the whites of his eyes and teeth showing under a dull patina of coal dust—had just come through the furnace room door as I filled the furnace hoppers with coal.

The furnace supplied steam heat and hot water for the six apartments on the top three floors and the janitor's apartment in the basement on the other side of the furnace room: that was us, the janitors, free rent and free phone. I was the janitor starting in 6th grade. And in addition I soon became the *shabbas goy*, the neighborhood gentile errand boy, the odd job kid.

Dad put his lunch box on the workbench, pulled off his boots.

"Where did you get that watch?"

"Boodman."

"You mean the landlord?"

"Yea Boodman. He was waiting for me on the front porch. He says it was his present for Bar Mitzvah. You know what that is?"

"It's like our confirmation."

"He wants you to have the watch."

"He wants me to have it! Why?"

"Yea why? Finish the furnace. We can talk later. I have to get ready for a job tonight right after supper, digging up Bronstein's sewer pipe."

I swept up and started shoveling again. Emmanuel Jesus Boodman owned the building, drove a Buick, smoked top cigars and lived downtown in the fashionable German Hotel. I had spoken with him once. He stopped me as I cut the grass to say that he heard I was a good worker. Then he asked what I was going to do in life.

"The mines like your father? I hear you're not a good student, really bad grades."

"Bad grades. I don't care about grades. We need money and school is not about money."

"So what are you going to do?"

"I don't know. But not the mines."

"What about college?"

"I don't know what they do in college. Beside I hear it takes money. We don't have money."

Finished with the coal, I shoveled the ashes out of the bottom of the furnace and rolled the ash cans out to the curb.

Then up the stairs to collect the garbage. I dumped one can per apartment into a big can, then on the second floor I took a break; sat on the steps out of breath. Occasionally I had been coughing up black coal dust. I had seen miners—old at 55 with the black lung—struggling to breathe. One of the tenants might wander by: "Oh my, aren't we hard workers."

I looked through the magazines the tenants threw out. Mrs. Byerly threw out the *Look* or *Life* which often had a picture of a medical doctor with a stethoscope endorsing cigarettes on the back cover. She was good for 50 cents a week when I would scrub her kitchen floor. (Her hulking son would often sit watching me and comment: "Richie I love to watch you work"). Mrs Ungas, 2nd floor West, paid me 50 cents to wash her windows.

Mrs Berkowitz, 2nd floor East, would pay me to run to the store. Once she sent me to Memelstein's to get liver for her cat. This was wartime when any meat was scarce. Mom—surprised to hear that Mermelstein had liver—sent me back for some to cook with onions for supper. I pointed to the liver in the butcher case.

"Mom wants me to get one pound of liver."

"Vee don haf no lifer."

"But I just got some for Mrs Berkowitz."

"Vee don haf no lifer."

"But I see it right there in the case."

"Vee don haf no lifer."

So soup again for dinner.

When I got back from the garbage run, Dad was soaking in a tub of very hot water that turned him bright red. At 130 pounds he was always cold and craved heat. Every day at this time I'd sit on the toilet seat while Dad—through a cloud of steam—would tell me about the mines, the explosions, the mules that were born in the mines and never saw any light but the miners' lamps, how the miners worked in four-foot-high chambers where they had to lie on their sides to shovel, the rats, their little red eyes reflecting the miners' lamps in the blackness as they waited for a crumb to drop from the miners' lunch, the communal toilet which was a ditch that ran down the middle of the gangway (hall). Or being wet all day or cold or both and the religious experience of coming up the shaft in the cage (elevator)—still alive—and seeing daylight again or a starlit sky in winter and breathing air—free of black coal dust. But tonight he tried to make sense of the watch.

"As far as I know, the tenants probably told Boodman about all the work you do around here."

A vegetable soup—a free soup bone if Mom bought a few withered vegetables from the grocery at closing time—was bubbling on the stove. The smell of freshly baked bread—cooling on the cupboard—mixed with the odor of strong coffee perking on the hissing, crackling coals of the huge black iron stove. At supper we passed the watch around.

Dianne, my kid sister asked:

"Why is Hitler putting people like Boodman in jail? Mrs. Isaac pays for my

YMCA swimming lessons and Mrs Tiov for my ballet lessons."

Dad took one last gulp of coffee, lit his pipe, put on his cap and went out into the rain.

"I don't know, but I have to fix Bronstein's sewer."

As Mom cleaned the table I ate everything that was left in all the bowls on the table: beans, rutabaga, turnips, greens. Mom laughed.

"Eat up Bud, you never know where your next meal is coming from."

I ran through the rain to Bronstein's to hold the flashlight and umbrella for Dad as he dug.

"Richard the umbrella, I'm getting soaked."

GOODBYE SHINGLETOWN

We were lucky to be here on the HILL even if it meant living in a janitor basement apartment. We had moved here from Shingletown, a collection of miners' dwellings close to the Diamond Mine where Dad worked before being laid off due to the Depression.

Back in Shingletown every night at 5 PM the radio announced the mine work schedule for the next day.

"MileDeep not working. Diamond mine day shift only."

From experience I knew by the age of 5 that if the Diamond was working we could expect some thing other than soup and bread for dinner.

Outside of Gauldiri's corner Mom and Pop grocery—on upended soda boxes—sat some of Shingletown unemployed, unskilled laborers: miners, roofers, house painters, from all over Europe with newspapers in the soles of worn out shoes and patches on trousers.

Back then may have been short on money and food but not on company. It seems that all our relatives wound up living with us at one time or another during the Depression. Uncle Mert would sneak in late at night smelling of beer and limburger cheese and climb into the communal bed with me and maybe

Uncle Dylan or other relatives. Mom would throw them out if she heard of them spending money on tobacco or beer. She was a non-smoker, non-drinking severe Welsh Baptist and condemned those who wasted money on non-essentials. But they felt useless without work, and ashamed of not bringing home a paycheck. A little beer helped. So they were thrown out often only to be let back in after what seemed to be a suitable period of penance. These were all from my mother's side. My father's family—just as needy—were too terrified of Mom's acid tongue to join the menagerie of the down and out.

Aunt Melva, Mom's youngest sister—now a young and pretty woman—slept on the couch.

In the evening Melva—if she was lucky enough to have a shop girl job at a store downtown—would iron her work dress while the radio played The World Turns and her hand rolled cigarette smoldered in an empty tuna fish can.

Aunt Melva helped Dad to make the aprons and bake the bread he sold door to door in the neighborhood.

Was Melva my real mother? Would that explain the powerful magnetism that drew me to Melva from earliest memory, or throw light on the way my mother treated me? Was it more than just a rumor?

I recall one Sunday when I was about 5 we were to go to the river on a picnic. My father's friend had a car and as Melva and I waited—excited about riding in a car and picnic food—a heavy spring downpour. Big fat drops. A knock on the door. A telephone message from Gauldiri's corner store: picnic rained out. My eyes moistened. Melva held me, consoled me. I still feel the warmth of her embrace.

Or it could've been that Ma chose the wrong parents.

Minni and Brendan Hughes left the coal fields of Wales for the mines of Scranton where after some years he—already with Black Lung—got TB and died leaving 7 children. The bank took the house; they moved into a cold water flat in Patagonia—the Welsh section of town. Minnie pushed the pram with baby Melva across town to do housework. One winter evening Minnie came home with Melva in her arms. She had traded the pram for bread and peanut butter. Then in winter's cold the finance company took the stove, the only warmth in the house. Soon after, Minnie died. The 7 kids slept fully clothed all together for warmth. The oldest was Dye at 15 who tried house painting, roofing. Next was Blodwin at 14 to keep house. Ma at age 12 quit school; went to work at the silk mill.

Whatever she did to us she would say: "it's for your own good."

But ... Honor thy father and mother.

If Dad wasn't pushing aprons or bread he was hiking the mountain that flanked the coal fields reciting poems as he walked; poems from poetry books gleaned from used book stores. Sometimes he would take me along and even at five years old I was expected to keep up.

"Richie watch out for that rattler."

Mom found out—probably at the local Welsh Baptist Church—that the Department of Agriculture would include free seeds with the commodity foods so we had a large supply of tomatoes, potatoes, squash, string beans. A free soup bone from the butcher and you had a great soup. The cucumbers we ate with vinegar and bread warm from the oven. The rhubarb went into pies.

Ma—while reading the Dear Abby column—would stab the air with her index finger "we need to get away from these low lifers."

THE HILL

Ma had found out about a janitor apartment on the HILL from Gordon the guy with the car from the mines.

"Nice people, lots of odd jobs and plenty of housework. No down and outs hanging round."

Dad called from the pay phone at Gauldieri's. Then we walked across town to talk to the owner Emanual Jesus Boodman. He was impressed with Dad's mechanical background and his knowledge of big boilers (furnaces in the mines that made the steam that powered the underground trains and the elevators). So we got the janitor's apartment on the Hill on Myrtle Street, free rent, and free telephone which was almost never used since we didn't know anyone who had a telephone that we could call. I was told not to use it.

(Later—when no one was looking—I would pick it up and listen to Itzy. Itzak Utan was on our party line—multiple houses but one number. Sometimes I would listen to him talk with high school friends about girls. If he heard me breathing, he would shout "Richie get off the phone.")

We walked across town to the Hill hauling rags, mops, a bucket and the usual peanut butter and homemade bread. Dad fired up the coal stove in the kitchen while Ma started scrubbing the grime from the windows. Dianne and I pitched in till Dianne said we should go and see where the school was. She was about to start first grade and I would be in fourth. We started up Myrtle Street, the crisp autumn air with the odor of burning leaves: shiny automobiles in the driveways, pretty houses with grass. Right out of a picture book. Ma said rich people lived here. After a few blocks we saw a sign announcing Petersburg: a bank, a 10 cent store, grocery, a shoemaker and an ice cream parlor. We didn't know what Mom meant by rich people but we knew what ice cream meant.

A deep orange October sun was sliding behind the west mountain as we found our way back to the basement apartment where Ma and Dad were waiting to start our hike back to Shingletown for the last time.

FLOWERS DON'T GROW IN THE COAL MINES

I enrolled in the 4th grade at Madison School where one day I noticed that a girl was watching me shoot marbles. Later she asked me if I could visit her at her house. That Saturday I walked up the hill to the Goldfarb house. Ma insisted Dianne—now in first grade—go with me. Mrs Goldfarb—tall and slim, wearing a flowered dress with her hair in a boyish cut—stood waiting on the veranda with Cele—my classmate—and younger sister Joan. Like her mother Cele was slender and tall for her age and like her mother she wore a flowered dress that showed black patent leather shoes over calf-high white socks. Joan was similarly dressed. Except for size they could have been taken for triplets. They led us—on the veranda which surrounded the house—to the rear and down the steps onto a manicured lawn bordered by freshly planted annuals, a checkered table cloth and a wicker picnic hamper.

Mrs Goldfarb poured milk into delicate glasses and served quartered sandwiches of cucumbers and cream cheese on white or tuna salad on wheat. There were pickles and olives on small white plates. A smile began to form on her lovely oval face as she watched us devouring the food and looking wide eyed at the small cakes that lay on a plate at the edge of the picnic cloth.

"You're not drinking your milk!"

"We don't drink milk."

"Would you like soda instead?"

"No. We drink water or coffee."

"And what does your father do Richard?"

"He works in the mines."

"The mines, you mean underground. You mean he coal mines?"

"The mines and Mom cleans houses."

A long pause: "Oh I see. So where did you go to school before Madison?"

"I went to Montgomery School in Shingletown.

"Shingletown?"

"Where the coal miners live."

"I see. Well how did you get to live here on the Hill?"

"Gordon, another miner, told Dad about a janitor apartment here on Myrtle Street."

Dianne chirped "We live in the janitor's basement apartment of a big building on Myrtle St. Richard does the janitor work."

"Richard you are the janitor?"

"He fills the coal furnace, takes out the ashes, the garbage, shovels the snow, cuts the grass."

"Oh I see. Well, uh yes. Well why don't you and Dianne come on Saturday. We can all eat lunch together?"

"Ok, but we better go now. I need to do chores before Dad gets home."

Walking home Dianne said "I wish we could live there."

That Saturday we were led through an oak-paneled living room lined with books and a fireplace between leaded glass windows to a sunlight breakfast room where we had lunch—hot dogs and orange soda.

Then I overheard Cele's mother say over the phone that she was looking for someone to help with light housekeeping and cooking.

"My Mother can do that and she is always looking for work."

The following Saturday it was my Mom that served the hot dogs and orange soda.

* * *

Not far from our new home on the Hill was the German mansion, a relic—like so many other deserted mansions—from the days when anthracite coal was king. It's eyeless windows looking down through the drizzle as the evening lights lit up in the Valley below.

Trash had been thrown in its extensive gardens. A refrigerator box offered cover. Dianne and I backed into the box and watched the darkness settling in. Finally she said:

"Lets go."

"Not yet. Let's wait till Dad gets there."

EASY TIMES

On an easy summer evening the Petersburg Street car wheels squeal as it turns left off Pine Street into Quincy to stop in front of Workman's Corner: Julius Workman's kosher market-deli, brother Sheldon's pharmacy/soda fountain/sweet shop and finally oldest brother Saul's cleaning establishment. Saul tall, elegantly dressed, a Panama hat shielding his handsome face against the late sun leaned against the door of the cleaners nursing a cigar. In the front window of his house right next door we might get glimpses of his beautiful wife who—it was whispered—was a gentile.

Snap Nagelman took bets on the upcoming Scranton Red Sox game. Kids licked ice-cream cones or chugged root beer floats from the soda fountain dispensed by Benny in a white apron. The smell of tomorrow's bagels from the oven.

And there was stick ball in the alley where we would use a broom handle to hit a tennis ball and run bases. Or we would make a football out of a large tomato can wrapped in newspaper held together with bailing wire and play touch football. Often Mrs. Sternfeld would lean out the 3rd story window, "Freddy go to Mermelstein, get a fresh bread."

When there was fresh snow, after supper we would get the Flexible Flyer out of the furnace room and drag it to the Pine Street Hill about four blocks away. Ma loved sledding. She would sit in front, Dianne right behind.

"Push, Richard push."

I would give it a shove and jump on. Whoosh. Then haul it back up. Finally, half frozen we would head home and drink hot water or if lucky, hot cider.

CATHEDRAL SCHOOL

I finished at Madison, the local grade school and transferred to the Cathedral School, the Catholic school downtown. I knew a lot of those kids from summers at the swimming pool. Days at Cathedral were happy. We all felt that we belonged there. Maybe it was because we shared the same religious rituals and similar working class culture.

A priest from the Cathedral School started giving basketball training. I had an old shaggy pair of canvas Converse sneaks, good enough, but I had seen a pair of leather top basketball shoes in the window at the sporting goods store. I wanted them. I didn't really need them but I wanted them. Very expensive at the time. I pictured myself leaping off the floor making baskets in my leather tops as the crowd cheered. I saved from my odd jobs and janitor work. Finally I went in to buy them but they were a size too big—an inch of space in front of the toe.

"You'll grow into them," he said.

By now with all the saving, the anticipation of wearing these expensive shoes at practice, the anticipated approval of classmates, the guilt I felt over spending so much money on what I didn't need, like leather top gym shoes, and against my intuition I bought them.

"You'll grow into them," he said.

Summer came and I was working at the park running the popcorn machine plus my usual janitor's work. No time for basketball but I wore my leather top gym shoes proudly everyday.

Summer over. All my classmates had grown. My feet had not, neither had I. With my too big leather top shoes I sat out the season on the bench.

If you don't need it, you don't want it.

But it was just as well, since that October Mom went back to work at the mill. I had to walk downtown again to walk Mom home at 8pm since she was afraid to walk home alone in the dark.

Graduation was approaching. Bebo Stranko was saying, "if we're gonna survive out there we need exposure to the real world—not just kids from the working class, not just Catholics."

So we decided on Central High, not South Catholic.

The first day in algebra class, I chose a seat in the front row to better see the drawings on the blackboard. The teacher Mrs. Carr leaned over my desk and suddenly started sniffing.

"What's that I smell. What have you got in your hair?"

"Vaseline," I answered.

Laughter.

If I went home with one of my new classmates I was often asked where I lived, what did my father do, what church did I go to.

The janitor's basement apartment, the mines, the Cathedral: not the answers to get invited back.

One day as I was digging for my lunch through the stuff at the bottom of my locker I was pulled upright by my shirt collar. It was Gingy.

"What's in the lunch kid, gimme that bag. Oh no, not peanut butter again. Wait. Is that your mother's Welsh shortbread ? I'll take it."

Gingy Weiss was one of the many that had quit High School and—being big—lied about their age and joined the WWII Army to see action and in the hopes of maybe escaping the coal mines. They had done the bars and bordellos of Europe and Asia and now were in school with kids just recently out of short pants.

BOOT CAMP

I borrowed $20 from Dad for some high school expense.

"Last week I loaned you $20. They are hiring for the evening shift at the furniture factory next to Roaring Brook."

I worked in the furniture factory at night after school from 6pm–10 pm. A two-mile hike to school and another two miles home, fill the furnace, take out the ashes, collect the garbage, hike to the factory. After two weeks I had enough to pay the loan.

"Here's your money."

For Dad all of life was boot camp, preparation for survival.

What made sense to me was making money now. I didn't connect the dots between high school and making money. To connect the dots we need to know where the dots are, what the dots do.

Next to the University stood the ivy-mantled exclusive Century Club. Emblazoned on the door was the Club's mission statement:

"For 105 years, the Century Club of Scranton has been a resilient power source in the Electric City saluting the past, embracing the present, and cultivating the future."

Membership by invitation only.

I heard that the hat check girl for the Century Club dance was sick. I got the job.

No instructions.

I had positioned a dish on the counter with bills in it. As the dancers filed in with their dates, we took the coats and I held up two fingers.

After a pause: "two dollars!"

"Right."

Not happy but they paid it, except from Jerry Coins. He lived in one of the big houses across from the Park, father executive at the local electric company. He said:

"Isn't that a lot?"

"This is the Century Club. Right? It cost a lot to join and there's the monthly dues. So what's two bucks?"

The following week Jerry's father called my mother saying he wanted to see me.

"Now what have you done Richard?"

That Saturday evening I was shown into the wood-paneled library, book shelves between leaded glass windows and a fireplace. I was shown to a chair where I sat awaiting Mr Coins' entrance.

"Well, so you're the Richie that charged your colleagues $2 for hat check. You were lucky to even see the inside of the Century Club. An exclusive club. Membership by invitation only.

"So here's where it stands. Give the money back. Donate it to the club. Do you understand?"

"I do understand. My father is a coal miner. Ma cleans houses. We live in a janitor's basement apartment where I do the janitor work. That's what I understand. Good night."

After a few months I mentally dropped out of Central and concentrated on neighborhood handyman jobs—where I picked up some cash—or instead of school—tramping in the nearby woods or swimming in Roaring Brook or the quarry ponds that filled with rain water in the spring.

Eventually I was suspended and Ma had to go to talk with the principal.

Summer came. I worked the popcorn machine or the cotton candy machine at the park all summer, always giving Mom half.

"Richard's a good boy," as she stuffed the bills in her apron pocket.

WASHING DISHES IN THE POCONO MOUNTAINS

The last day of freshman year Dad said after supper we need to get up early. So at 5am, I made the eggs and coffee and we headed out to the truck. (Dad had just gotten a truck. The war called for ever more coal which meant overtime money in the paycheck.) The entire back of the pickup was filled with a big bundle covered with a tarp.

"What's that?"

"You'll see."

"Where are we going?"

"You'll see."

After about 45 minutes on leafy backroads we arrived at Lake Wallenpaupack, turned off the lake road onto a dirt road into the woods and untied the bundle: a big pole in two sections. The bottom section maybe 8 inches in diameter.

What's this?

"A tent. This is the garbage dump for the resorts on the Lake. You're camping here for the summer. I'll be back next Saturday."

"But the furnace, the ashes, the garbage."

"It's summer so no need to fill the furnace every night. I'll take care of it."

Not unusual. It seemed we never talked about anything, especially about what to do to make our lives better. I always seemed to have the idea that we could do better, get Ma out of this basement apartment if we could just talk about it. Both my parents were smart but not logical. Those smarts were never used to talk about improving our lives.

One example: the dining room table. Mom was often telling us about the beautiful furnishings in the homes she cleaned. So one day the department store delivered a dining room table and chairs and set it up in the kitchen. Because this was a basement apartment the radiators were on the ceiling centered over the table was a huge metal radiator. The one window looked out at pavement level into the alley showing Shulowitz's garage on the other side. The table took up most of the room in the kitchen. It belonged in a large dining room not in a janitor's basement kitchen under a radiator.

Did we talk about it? Did any one ask about it? No. No one mentioned it even though it was totally out of place. Public school boards don't want the students to ask questions, to ask for evidence.

"Do you believe in the gods?"

"The gods. Where are they?"

"The gods are everywhere."

"Everywhere? Then why can't I see them?"

"You don't have to see them, you must believe in them."

The truck pulled away. Alone on a dump for a week. Morning breezes, the odor of the lake, of pine trees, of coffee. The solemn stillness of summer afternoons. Scavenging fire wood, clear water from a stream, dinner cooking on pine branches, golden sunsets. The gathering darkness, fading embers, fireflies, moonlight. It could be worse.

Sure enough on Saturday the truck pulled up about 10am.

"I've got a job for you down at the Lake."

Across the Lake Road at the White Beauty View Resort we were met by the smiling robust Naldo, the owner. "So the boy you told me about. I hear you good worker. Ok. See that door. That's the kitchen. Tell Rosa, I sent you. You are the new dishwasher."

Rosa, well fed, jolly: "Bambino, You eat at the counter, whatever you want, 3 meals, snacks whatever. When you finish here at 5 or 6 or whenever, you go over to the drive-in to Joe. He will tell you how to usher in the cars."

Soon all of Naldo's family came by to see the new kid. They were happy; they were kind; they liked to eat, they talked. They laughed at the Irish bambino. I had found a home.

After a couple of days, two guys—groundskeepers—a few years older than me, came to look me over. After a little talk they showed me a tent behind the main lodge where they bunked.

The next day they came by.

"You can move in with us. No good alone at the dump in that tent."

The next morning—and every morning for the rest of the summer—I woke up to the sounds of Tommy Dorsey. They only had one record and that was Dorsey's jitterbug classic "In the Mood."

Tony, the youngest of Naldo's family, had a key to the liquor locker. One night about 9pm I had my first taste of what they called chianti; a mixture of ginger ale and red wine which Vince had swiped from the liquor locker. I woke up late to the usual "In The mood" and felt sleepy all day. So at noon after lunch I lay down under a tree. Naldo himself woke me up.

"Bambino why you no wash dishes?"

"I'm resting, I need a nap to digest my lunch. You don't want me to get ulcers do you?"

He laughed and helped me up.

School was to start on the following Monday so I arranged with the milk man from Scranton for a ride back to town. Home after an hour, I scrambled some eggs and lay down to rest. I woke up the next day about 10am. I had slept more than 24 hours.

Sophomore year, so we stayed out later. But not much later. One night I got home at 11pm. There was something blocking the door. When I finally was able open it I found Dad sitting in a chair with his feet against the door.

Usually a bunch of us would go to the YMCA downtown where there was a Friday evening dance. Chic Checkers would hold open the door to the gym (scene of the dance), look inside at the girls through a cloud of Skin creme.

"There's nothing here." So we went downstairs to the pool, swam and then went to the diner where we played pinball.

CHASING GOLF BALLS AT SKYTOP LODGE

Schools out. I could have gone back to White Beauty View on the Lake with the glow of the warm Italian family but I liked the idea that I survived by myself among strangers that last summer, so why not go see what else is out there. As usual, too naive to be afraid, believing in luck. Maybe counting on credits I might have with whatever gods there may be.

Back on the highway, thumb out. A sticky summer day; a slight drizzle dampened the wool coat sweater I borrowed from my father. Now it reeked a wet wool smell. The too-long rolled-up sleeves being damp were falling down and the sweater neck scratched me. Then a car pulled over.

I got out at Canadensis, a small mountain village and celebrated my progress by drinking coffee in the drugstore. Then I hiked the miles to SkyTop. I crossed a bridge over the stream that watered the golf course to see the Lodge majestically atop the mountain against a perfect spring sky: a fairy tale castle.

It looked down over a blue lake—rippled by the breeze—ringed by forested mountains. Built just before the Great Depression it had massive fireplaces, dining rooms, two swimming pools, an 18-hole golf course and a ski run. The sun was low as I found my way around the lake to the caddy tent camp where I was met by Wanda, a youngish woman, the caddy master's wife, the camp boss and cook. She showed me the showers and toilets, the mess hall and assigned me to an army style cot in the bunk house. I had missed supper so she gave me some left over beans and hot dogs. I would see a lot of beans and dogs in the weeks ahead. Then I sat by the Lake watching the evening settle in.

In the morning I awoke to the sounds of the caddies turning out. I was by far the youngest there. Rusty—who took me under his wing—could have been 30 but to me at 14 he looked like an old man.

Breakfast—included in the $9/week—was eggs, toast, coffee. Oatmeal optional. I followed the crowd to the caddy shack next to the lake. A rustic building with benches along the wall. A large sign read NO GOLF CARTS ALLOWED on the course so the only recourse was to pay a caddy or carry your own bag. Soon the golfers arrived; the caddy master sent the caddies out until I was alone on the bench. About lunch time—Wanda the kitchen goddess came by with a sandwich and an apple. saying "this is not to be an everyday event." Then two golfers showed up. I was the only one left so out I went a bag on each shoulder. The caddy master whispered "these guys are green so just see where the ball goes." A double loop—two bags—for 18 holes was worth $2 a bag. Big money in 1948. So I carried about 30 pounds for about 2 miles. The golfer would say "where's the ball?" "Hunh, ball? They just laughed and gave me a fat tip.

A few days and I was able at least to know where the ball landed. When asked which club I would say "for this fairway it doesn't matter."

The caddy rules at SkyTop: no talking—under any circumstances—to the children of the guests, no loitering around the lodge and no going into the lodge. The exception was that on movie night when the lodge showed a movie in the main room. Caddies were allowed to sit on the floor in front of the seats. I usually went as an alternative to watching the evening settle in—again.

When I got comfortable with my new life I started going to Strouds-burg—a pretty town in the east foothills of the Poconos—because I had heard of a Friday evening dance at the Y. I hitched hiked or if enough cash on hand I took the train.

After a few Fridays at the Y I met Justine and danced with her regularly and eventually walked her home through the leafy streets of modest well kept homes.

It became my fantasy to live in one of the houses—above ground not in the janitor's basement—with a front porch swing where I could rock and watch Stroudsburgers wander by. Justine became the main character in my Stroudsburg fantasy.

After walking her home I would meet Jackie another caddie from SkyTop at a prearranged corner where there was an institutional looking building that had a hammock in the backyard way back from the building. Jackie would lie down in one direction and I in the other, our legs overlapping.

"Jackie your smelly socks are in my face."

We woke up with the morning dew and headed to the train station with a stop in the diner for a coffee.

This great job, open air, walking—my favorite meditation therapy—trees, grass, the mountain breeze, a swim in the lake to finish off the day and no nagging, came to an end with the start of my junior year at Central High.

The first summer day—at the end of my junior year—back on the highway thumb out. I was heading to a Pocono resort—Winn Lake Lodge—I had heard about from Mr. Sussman, one of my neighbors, who said it kept kosher and I would be treated well. They had just lost the day shift dishwasher and hired me when I told them about my summer at White Beauty View. My bunk was the lower level of a two-decker bunk in the kitchen. Everyone was pleasant and very very well fed. The sport here was not on the tennis court or in the pool, it was in the dining room and some of these guests might be Olympic champs. When not eating they were waiting to eat, dozing in sunny mountain air.

The second Friday as I was busing tables I hoisted a tray of champagne glasses above my shoulder waiter style and as I walked to the kitchen I slipped. All the glasses fell and broke on the floor. The maitre'd came toward me wagging his finger, "the fish wagon," "the fish wagon"—and pointing to one of the waiters—"you too, the fish wagon." Many of the guests got up from the table and started stuffing bills in our hands, fives, ones.

The fish wagon was a utility vehicle used among other things to get supplies from the train. We were to be dropped at the train station. The fish wagon was the worst thing that could happen to an employee, almost like a dishonorable discharge from the military, but I was happy to leave my bunk in the kitchen. The fish wagon driver on the way to the train told me that his friend worked at the Honey Moon Lodge where they were looking for a *plongeur* (dishwasher) . After dropping the other fired waiter at the station he drove me there.

Honey Moon Lodge was a small lodge of individual cabins from the days when motels were separate cabins. There was no pool, no bar, some tennis courts, and a wide quiet stream that meandered close by the main building which included the dining hall behind which was the kitchen where I was to wash dishes and—in a pinch—bus tables.

Max and Cary—a live-in couple with a strong German accent—were the cooks. They supervised the women who lived locally and worked the meal times. I was served meals on a small table about the size of a large pizza which was also the office where they kept all the bills and invoices as well as their medicines and smelly food leftovers spoiling in the mountain heat. For company I had some local flies leaving their deposits on all of the above and on my food if I didn't shoo them off. It was difficult to eat there because all of this stuff gave me a stomach ache but I did have an appetite and ate quickly. I don't know where Max and Cary ate so I asked Cary if I could eat at another table.

"Vat you want. You tink you paying guest?"

So nothing changed except the number of flies as the weather cooled with the approach of Autumn.

I would sit with the groundskeeper Alfred—a jolly old Brit—and his helper—a local kid about my age—by the stream evenings and listen to Alfred talk about his childhood in England. He had a 1934 Ford and every few weeks he would put us in the rumble seat and we would cruise along the leafy back roads to a roadhouse where Alfred would buy some beer and sneak us some so that we were asleep in the rumble seat by the time we got back.

Finally I was—with luck—to graduate.

At the graduation ceremony, as Mr. Veniello handed me the diploma he whispered, "This is the lowest graduating average ever awarded by Central High. Good luck in your new life." (Scranton style child psychology.)

DOOR TO DOOR

From the window of our basement apartment with the pavement at eye level I looked straight into Teddy Shulovitz's garage at his Caddy and Buick. As Teddy chewed a cigar I wandered into the alley:

"Richie whatcha gonna do now? You're out of high school. So what now? The mines like your father?"

"The mines? Not for me. I don't know. How about you give me a job in your brewery?"

"Good try but we are slowing down. Too many breweries around here now. Guengling giving us a hard time. I tell you what. Do like me: be a salesman, smoke good cigars, drive a Buick and be a salesman. I started out with Fuller Brush. Then you go bigger stuff from there."

So was I going to be a door-to-door peddler? That's how Teddy started and he was doing ok.

There was no pressure from schoolmates to do whatever or attend which ever college. I didn't have any schoolmates. It was clear to me that I was not one of the boys. The kids were either Jewish, me a Goy or they were well off, me living in a basement, father a coal miner, mother a housecleaner, or they were athletes or fraternity/sorority types, me the *shabbas goy* (handyman), janitor and window washer/floor scrubber. For me that was a real advantage: no expectations so no limits, no fear of failure.

Where to start? All I had was time and empty pockets. The day high school was out I signed on with Fuller Brush. On payday I smoked one of Teddy's cigars with Teddy in his garage. The Buick would have to wait. But Fuller Brush lasted only a month. I was not making enough money to even pay Mom room and board. But it taught me how to deal with the terror of knocking on doors: the mind numbing "cold canvass" as it is known in the trade.

There was an add for vacuum salesmen in the *Times*. The boss was a jolly Dutchman from Pennsylvania Dutch country. Zig Teigler gave us a brief training each Monday morning in his office downtown. We would dismantle a vacuum, reassemble it, then practice the monologue also known a the *spiel* or *schtick*. This included imagined questions and objections from the imaginary customer. Zig would say "Hit a door." We'd bang on an imaginary door and Zig playing the role of the house Frau would open the door. At that point we'd begin the schtick with Zig asking questions or making objections while we spouted canned responses we had memorized.

"Who's there?"

"It's me Richie."

"Yes."

"We are giving a free demo of this new FastWay vacuum. May I come in?"

"George there's a man here with a vacuum cleaner."

"We don't want one."

"Our old one is no good anymore."

"We don't want one."

"Come in and show me. George come see this demo."

"We don't need it."

"We do, the old one is shot."

"We can't afford it."

"It's ok. Show me. George come look at this."

So then does George throw me out or do we get to demo?

Then there was marketing. We watched the obituaries looking for obits of miners who died from black lung or a mining accident. That meant that the widow had received insurance money and maybe could afford a new vacuum.

There I met two seasoned door-to-door salesmen, guys who had done aluminum siding, roofing, aluminum windows, insurance, mutual funds. Anything that would sell door-to-door. Mike Tomeo was a sweet little Italian who had a '49 Chevy sedan and Jerry O'Connell who—cursed with the drink as they say—had a bulbous alcoholic nose like WC Field with pink thread veins. We all rode in Mike's Chevy; Jerry and I split the gasoline costs. For some reason we always wound up on the leafy back roads up in the Pocono foothills. Sometimes Mike brought along his guitar and a lunch his wife packed which we shared. Mike would then find a shady spot and after lunch he would play Italian peasant songs and we would nap in the cool air.

Once we had exhausted the obituary column in the *Times* we had to cold canvass—knock on doors.

Two guys would hit a door and if they got in, do the demo and if lucky split the commission. This was the 'Fifties when people would open the door to a stranger in a small town.

The vacuum cleaner manager from the big city was in town and was hosting all the salesmen to a dinner at Carmella's, an out of the way Italian bistro where they say the Mafia hung out. That added some mystery to the event in addition to the promise of free restaurant food.

The big night arrived and although some of us were under 21, the big boss bought us a Miller High Life "the Champagne of Bottled Beer." The evening settled in as the beer and the background music loosened drowsy tongues. Then the big boss stood up and pointing to the loudspeaker above the bar, he challenged the crowd.

"Whoever can name that music gets a $10 bill."

I raised my hand; "it's Chopin's Polonaise."

"Right! but wait, what does a coal miner kid know about Chopin?"

"My mother saved enough Octagon Soap coupons to buy a phonograph but we only had one record: Chopin's Polonaise."

But there wasn't enough money in vacuum cleaners either. The Lackawanna Valley people were poor. I could hardly pay Ma rent.

READER'S SERVICE TRAVELING BOOKSTORE

In the local paper I read an add: "Florida in the winter, California in the summer, see the US, earn and save money under supervision of Reader Service staff." I applied, I liked the Boss, Vic Moskowitz and he hired me on the spot.

I told my folks that I was going to work with Reader Service (RS) and sell books door to door; that I would be going to Florida and even California. They only had a vague notion where these places were since the furthest they had gone was Philadelphia. To them it probably sounded like my overly active imagination. I don't remember any words from them as I headed out. I always had the feeling that I was expected to leave once out of high school anyway. Another mouth to feed.

I took the trolley to Wilkes-Barre, about a 20 mile ride. The hotel was in a sketchy part of town. The desk clerk told me that the boss Vic Moskowitz was not in and that I was to go to a certain room. Once there the door was opened by Mick Duckworth. A big pudgy guy. We shook hands and he told me which side of the bed was mine unless Murray came back, then I would be in the middle.

Mick was from Smallton, West Virginia, which according to him was the bordello of Appalachia. He had the accent of a country western singer and enjoyed telling me stories about Smallton and his travels with Reader Service. As is often the case in hotels of this sort where the bathroom was down the hall there was sink in the room. Mick was washing his hands with his back to me and suddenly he turned and threw something on the bed. It looked a large marble. Then Mick laughed and said "it's my eye, my glass eye."

Great way to start a new career: Three in the bed and one with a glass eye. I wanted to go home. But . . .

The next morning we went to a meeting where all the crews were assembled. Crews consisted of 3 to 5 including a "manager" depending on how big a car the manager had. The guys who bought a used limo (usually a Desoto) from Vic would have room for a crew of 5.

There were about 25 young men and women in the large room, some with white shirts, ties and sport jackets. Vic introduced the new guy, me and then started the Monday morning training with the spiel. Each one stood and went through the pitch (aka spiel) demonstrating the books as they spoke. Vic would interrupt with customer comments, questions he had heard in his early days on the street.

"Well I better ask my husband if it's ok."

I did not yet know the spiel but I would before the day was over. Then we heard a report from one of the crew managers on Dale Carnegie's *Power of Positive Thinking*. Another got up to talk about Ziggie Zigler who coined the phrase "sell the sizzle not the steak." Ziggie was the salesman's patron saint, required reading.

Once the crews were gone Vic handed me the written spiel and told me to memorize it so I could recite it by noon. I did. We had a bowl of soup in the hotel coffee shop then he handed me the book samples. I was to weave the book demo into the spiel. I was about to perform for him when the crews came back. Each reported the day's sales for the crew and for crew members. Then everyone went down to the coffeeshop for dinner which was often beans and hotdogs, Mac and cheese, pasta or hamburgs with coffee to wash it down. Then back up to Vic's big room for the cool down: talk about how to improve sales, the pitch etc. And which town we go to next. There was some excitement in the crowd when Vic explained that next month we would break for Christmas and meet again in sunny warm Miami, a big improvement over the Wilkes-Barre, Pennsylvania winter cold.

The next day I went out with one of the crew managers, Seymour Badin, and watched him pitch some real live people and make a few sales. Then I tried it and made a lot of mistakes. Finally I dropped the sample book on the ladies foot, but the lady laughed and actually bought it when Sy explained I was a trainee. That evening I was a celebrity at the meeting as the first new guy that made a sale on the first day.

The next day I went out again with Sy but this time we did "block around" meaning I went in one direction, he in another until we met in someone's house. The meet-up usually happened when the door opened and we saw the other team member inside.

At the Pep rally the next morning Vic, the boss, repeated the info about Miami. Adding that those who had no place to go could stay in the hotel here in

Wilkes-Barre or in Scranton and they would be picked up for the trip to Florida. Then he surprised us all: I was to drive one of the 1949 DeSoto limousines, drop off the team members who lived locally, take the limo back to Scranton and after Christmas pick up local team members for the trip to Florida. We were surprised because I was only 17 years old and had only been with Vic for three weeks. So on Saturday night (we worked 6 days always) after dropping off the two locals, I surprised my parents in nearby Scranton by arriving in the limo. They were happy to see me but there was soon the unspoken nagging question in Ma's mind of how long I would be staying: the bad smell of the guest who might overstay their welcome. As usual I tried to gloss over the situation by resuming my janitorial duties and giving Mom some cash out of my "good side" for room and board. "Good side" was Reader Service lingo for savings which we usually deposited with Vic the boss. None of us understood compound interest anyway. And I took Mom to lunch at the "right places." Finally I picked up those who stayed in the hotel and we were off to sunny Florida.

I was the only driver. We slept in the car for 3 nights and smelled ripe after the second. Finally Miami, where Vic was relieved to see us. It was Saturday evening so we got to shower, sleep and rest on Sunday. Monday we were back on the street hitting doors.

We resumed our usual routine. The boss Vic would start the evening cool down spiel session with "hit a door" then he would become the customer:

"Suppose my husband doesn't like it, can I cancel and get my deposit back?"

"Oh sure just send a letter to the address on the receipt."

Sometimes a team member would play the customer. Mike Levy, a creative freckled redhead from Hells Kitchen, New York City, played four parts, the customer, Wanda Brown, her husband George, the neighbor lady across the street, Louise White and Mr White.

Mrs. White, the neighbor lady and her husband: "George I saw a strange man going into the Brown's house this afternoon and he was in there for quite a while."

George White and Mr. Brown: "Charley I'm trying out a new beer this weekend. Come on over and try it. By the way Louise tells me she saw a stranger in your house today and he was there quite a while. You getting something fixed?"

Mr. Brown and his wife Wanda: "Oh I meant to tell you but I've been so busy with supper. I bought this educational material. Here's the receipt and we can cancel it just with a letter."

The point of the scenario was to emphasize there may be a Louise peeking through the curtains.

Then one team member told of an experience in a suburban neighborhood on the outskirts of El Paso.

"I should call my husband to see if I should get this. He's a policeman."

"Ma'am you can tell him we are registered with the Chamber of Commerce under the name of Reader Service. Here is my license."

"Well ok. He said probably not."

"Thank you anyway."

After walking about a block a police car pulled alongside, a police man got out and snarled through clinch teeth "get in" as he held the back door open. He then got back into the passenger seat and said to the driver:

"I'm going to kill this kid as he brandished his revolver."

"Calm down. He's just a kid door-to-door salesman."

"Just a kid huh? Wasn't it just a kid posing as a salesman who raped a woman in Mobile? No way. I'm going to teach his kid a lesson."

"Put the gun away."

We later learned this is the good cop/bad cop routine.

Finished with Florida we moved on to Birmingham where I had a new roommate. Once again we were to share a bed. The class of hotel we stayed in only had double beds. Ivan Michael Mecklinberg was from the Henry Street Settlement in New York's Lower East Side where he lived with his Uncle Murray and his mother in a five-story walk up. Mike always had a phonograph with him and a small collection of classical records.

"Richie this is our best week. Let's celebrate. Uncle Murray always has a bottle of Manishevitz handy."

So we bought Manischewitz Concord Grape Kosher Wine.

We learned the hard way it is loaded with sugar. We had a kosher handover for work the next day. Kosher or no, a hangover is a hangover.

Galveston was tropical. Moist soft breezes off the Gulf, palm trees, endless summer.

West Texas. Endless space, tumble weeds, fences. cattle, space. Huge clouds rolling across the endless sky. A crossroads, a gas station, a mercado for groceries, farm supplies. In a cantina, a bonita señorita: almond eyes, shiny black hair and a smile that said:

"Take me with you, the big city."

San Angelo, Texas. A long day, few sales, a cold wind, a dark sky. Tired, hungry, I came upon a mom and pop gas station. The rest room: small, clean, warm, quiet. I sat on the toilet soaking up the comfort. A voice inside me said, I could live here; there's just enough room on the floor to lie down. I began to day dream/fantasize about how to set up a hot plate. I must have fallen into a sleep state: in my mind I was knocking on doors, making the pitch. Was I hallucinating? I ran outside and was glad to be back to reality even as it was.

Back outside the wind turned cold as evening settled in. Across the street the windows lit up in warm middle class homes, a housewife making dinner, a real dinner. I might call it a revelation, an epiphany, but I was struck with the realization that I was 18 years old and I was no place, had nothing, traveling with a bunch of unfortunates, poor like myself, who had few choices. Something had to change. But what? There was no going back to Scranton, so what were my choices? This. By default this was my choice. I had to make a financial success of this, of Reader's Service. But how? Become a crew manager. To do that I had to become a top producer, more sales, stop daydreaming, whining; then tell Vic I wanted a crew of my own. My parents had the car at home that I was supposed to be making payments on. Ok. A plan. Just then the crew manager drove up and we headed back to the hotel.

My crew manager was Pete Kawalski, maybe 23, smart, a top producer as was his pretty wife Donna. Pete was from the same Valley I grew up in, the Lackawanna Valley in Pennsylvania, Polish-American like some of my relatives. I could talk to Pete even though he treated me like his little brother. So after the cool down sales session that evening I went to his room and told him about my idea. He chewed on it for a while:

"Why not, but you need more sales."

His wife Donna with a motherly smile:

"I know you can do it, but better get some pizza money in the pocket first."

I felt they were laughing at me in a friendly way but now I was more determined that ever.

After we exercised I talked to Mike (Ivan Michael) about it. The question was what can we do to increase sales. Mike had just started reading Dale Carnegie's classic about positive thinking *How To Win Friends And Influence People*. To practice we told each other stories, stories that contained news that could be bad news or good news. The idea was to make it into good news.

"I had three doors in a row slammed in my face. But the 4th was a sale."

We turned out the lights feeling that we had taken a step in the right direction. Next evening during the usual cool down we introduced the idea to Vic. He liked it. Thereafter each evening someone would offer a story where they put a good—still realistic—spin on a situation of the day.

Next stop was to be Amarillo but on the way we blew a gasket in the 51 DeSoto Limo's straight 6 flat head engine. It was Sunday, we were in what looked like a desert with no other cars or buildings in sight. Just sand. When the gasket blew we were miraculously close enough to a gas station that we could push the limo in! What's more, it was open and even more:

"Y'all can use my tools and I can call my friend the DeSoto dealer and he will bring y'all a gasket."

"Even on Sunday?"

"Why not?"

Andy, Pete's brother—in spite of his Notre Dame BA degree—using tools from the gas station, was able to replace the gasket. We were on our way in about four hours.

After San Antonio we did Midland, and Odessa TX in the oil patch days. Everyone working. Easy sales. I hitchhiked one Sunday from Midland to Odessa to see the movie "Death of a Salesman," the story of a loser. It made me seriously question my future but now there was no turning back.

And my new determination was paying off. All of a sudden I was getting some recognition from the other crew managers, getting respect from Pete and Donna with less teasing abut pizza money.

During our weeks in El Paso we visited Juarez, Mexico. We thought of it as an exotic foreign country; I mailed a postcard to Elly my wannabe girlfriend back in my Valley. After a good run in Midland/Odessa we spent a week in Carlsbad, New Mexico and then Phoenix and at last California. The iron rice bowl. San Diego, 1952 was a sleepy town with a picante salsa ambiance. Look west at the Pacific, east at the mountains, up at the ever present sun.

Fresno in the spring heat. Humid, flat. We had a three-day holiday here so to celebrate we played baseball in a local park under the blazing sun. It was so humid we took off our shirts and drank the apple juice that Donna had brought along. Try knocking on doors while subject to violent diarrhea attacks with no public toilets close by.

Oakland. The road to San Jose from Oakland was Mission Boulevard, a two lane road whose only building was a gas station about half way to San Jose.

Then San Francisco where we checked in to the Commodore Hotel on Sutter Street.

At the top of a hill we could see the Pacific in the distance.

"Mike this is my new home, this most beautiful city. One more trip to Pennsylvania to tell my folks about it and then I return."

One of the crew members was Merle Cannon from Mississippi. Movie star handsome, with a chiseled face and graying blonde hair and a charming southern drawl. In San Francisco I roomed with him. I watched him immerse his skinny body into a tub of steaming water, sip a glass of gin he placed on the side of the tub and light a camel. He was to tell much later that he had done time in Mississippi State Prison for check forgery.

A crew member named Maye from Waco: the pleasant face we might find in a book about pioneers in the great plains. When we traveled the East Coast she would often for no reason let out a whooping:

"Ah ha, San Anton." Then announce "there's no scenery here." Nothing but a bunch of hills and mountains in the way so I can't see nothin. Back in Texas it's flat so you can see the scenery."

Most importantly she did well at sales, always one of the top producers.

Merle was not ambitious, content to make some money, set aside some good side (savings?), drink his gin, and smoke his cigarettes in a steaming tub of water at the end of the day. In Maye he saw security.

The wedding celebration was to start Saturday after work in the hotel bar. Most of the crew managers were there and some crew members. Most crew members did not drink nor did I. Sam a piano tuner from Lincoln, Nebraska, bought me a manhattan. It was sweet like soft drink. I drank it right down.

"Richie have another on me."

The manhattans kept coming but by now I had lost count and soon after I lost consciousness. I woke up for a short time in the back seat of the limo, everyone laughing, then passed out again. I was sick for a week with sticky sweet liquid oozing out of my gums. But I went to work everyday and made a decent amount of sales.

Then Portland, Oregon and finally Spokane where I jumped ship one Monday—after telling Vic and my manager Pete—taking a bus to the edge of town where I walked out on the two-lane highway 20 heading east. Too naive to be afraid.

THUMBING BACK TO SCRANTON

Time to go back to Scranton and tell my folks about the big world out there, how I would make enough money to get Ma out of the basement apartment, buy her a real house and then move back to San Francisco. But I soon found Route 20 was little traveled. I was getting rides ok but short rides, local people, rides on farm machinery. Finally a farmer picked me up.

"Sonny the East-West traffic is on Route 30. At this rate you'll be walking across Nebraska."

"Where is Route 30?"

"I will drop you at Chadron where you take the road going south. It's about 10 miles."

It was late afternoon when I first started down the linkage road to Route 30 but once again not much traffic. I just started walking and put out my thumb when I saw a car coming. But no luck and it was soon growing dark. Then it was pitch dark. No lights and little light from the cloudy sky. I could barely see the fences. Then as the evening wore on, my eyes grew accustomed to the dark and I could see there were cattle behind the fences and I began to imagine that they were following me on their side of the fence. Soon I was falling asleep on my feet. Then I saw the headlights of a car appearing and then disappearing on the hills as if riding the waves on a surf board . It was going north and I was headed south but a voice told me to get out of this dead end or I would soon be sleeping in the weeds. I crossed the road and put out my thumb. He stopped. The next thing I knew he woke me up.

"Sonny this is Worthington, Minnesota. There's a hotel. Good luck."

Next morning I awoke with the sun shining through the hotel window.

After a few good rides and a lot of truck stop food, I got a ride heading to Philadelphia. We slept in the truck at truck stops, me in the front seat and him in the sleeper behind me. Finally we had arrived in Philadelphia.

"I'm going to the Greyhound for a bus to Scranton."

"Not until you help me unload this truck."

At the next light I hopped out.

On the bus to Scranton I hammered the bus driver with stories of my travels.

"Scranton has the best water, Scranton's health drink. The first thing I will do when I get home is hook up the hose and drink my fill of that good mountain water."

I bet he was glad to see me go.

I called my folks from the bus station pay phone. They thought hitchhiking was risky but since I called from the bus station they thought I had taken the bus all the way. They were surprised since I had not phoned or written. (Long distance phone calls were too expensive.) I had been gone nine months.

I immediately resumed my janitor's role of the recent past, gave Mom some money, and announced that I would be leaving in two weeks, so as not to wear out my welcome.

With time on my hands at home I began to think about the Reader Service crews and realized that I missed them. I began to realize they were my family. They were not Catholic, they were not Irish or Welsh. Most of them were Jewish and probably had parents who were from eastern Europe or Germany. Some from Central, South America. But we ate, roomed together, traveled together, studied sales techniques, commiserated with each other as needed.

Most of them like me came from poor famlies, did not see any future for themselves except some menial job; for me that was the coal mines. Some were unwelcome at home or lived in an unwholesome household—alcohol, sexual abuse. And they had little education nor did they see any need for it. They need-ed money and there was a direct connection between door-to-door sales and money, not much money but more than they could make at home. They were not bad people, they were not immoral, not dishonest. They had good values but few choices. They were unskilled, not trained in how to connect the dots to improve their lives. Given the right parents they might have been world class pianists but they would never touch a piano, brilliant scientists but they would never take a science class. They had just picked the wrong parents.

But I had an advantage: My parents read poetry. Dad, even though he worked in he mines could still read Latin and French. Mom, forced to quit school in the seventh grade and work in the mill, read articles on healthy food, growing vegetables and about manners and she expected us to behave accordingly.

Dad was religious and we attended church. And maybe most important we lived on the Hill among decent, polite, educated people with whom we socialized in church and school and in the neighborhood. Very different street education than we would have gotten in Shingletown. If we still lived there I would probably have gone into the coal mines out of high school. My sister into the Mill. On the Hill I saw stable families in well kept homes. I heard classmates discuss college and careers, summer vacation, travel to Europe. I knew there was a better way. But how to get there?

Now I was eager to get back to work. Since my revelation that evening in San Angelo, my sales had picked up and I was getting recognition from the boss Vic. I phoned Vic and found he was in Denver, being careful to ask the long distance operator for the charges so I could leave money to pay Ma for the call. Long distance was considered a luxury for urgent needs only.

I said good-bye and took the Greyhound to Denver. It took three twenty four hour days with breaks in truck stops. I lost awareness after about eight hours but managed to eat something at each stop. I stared out the window at space as we cruised the Great Plains. All sorts came and went in the seat next to me. I was to be constipated for at least three days. Never again.

Vic sent one of the crew managers to pick me up at the bus station and the gang was happy to see me again. And I was happy to be home for now I realized that Reader Service had become my home and the crew members were my family. And Vic was our leader/father.

CREW MANAGER: Encyclopedia Road Show

Leaving Denver we headed East. Lincoln, Nebraska, Wichita, Kansas, Flint, Michigan, Kokomo, Indiana, Massillon, Ohio, Monongahela, Pennsylvania. Finally we were back in Scranton. Vic arranged to visit my parents and impressed them with my potential as a salesman and crew manager and my ability to make payments on the car.

I had become at age 19 a manager of three sales people (aka door-to-door peddlers). I got commission on each sale they made and a larger commission on my own sales.

Here was my chance to pay off the car and save money to get my parents out of that basement apartment and in to a normal house above ground. Back in San Angelo, Texas, I thought I was no place, had nothing. Now at age 19 I had a start.

I seemed to get the more educated new recruits. I had one guy from Baghdad, Iraq who had just finished a degree at Princeton. So why join up with a traveling book crew. He said it ensured he would see a slice of the real America, not the Hilton Hotel version, and there was security in the group and a guarantee of a hotel and food even if no sales.

A full year had passed. As a 19 year old I made $12,000 my first year as a manager. This was in 1953 when a good salary was $5,000 a year for a professional or skilled craftsman. After auto expenses, hotel costs, restaurants, etc. I saved $100 every week for 50 weeks and sent it home in a US postal money order addressed to my father. (Addressing to Dad would turn out to have been a mistake.) The idea was to provide enough money to buy land in the Pocono Foothills and enough used building material to build a real house above ground.

My folks bought a plot on Moosic lake in the foothills of the Pocono Mountains. Dad scavenged stuff from the mines including a junked water pump and a furnace which he repaired. He even cut the glass out of abandoned railroad car windows for the windows in the house. He hired a backhoe guy to dig the cellar. All the rest of the work Dad did himself except on the rare occasions when he needed more muscle. Then he would enroll some guys from the mines, supply a case of beer and some barbecue. After they helped hefting heavy beams or whatever, they would dip in the Lake to cool off and then—eating and drinking would spin yarns about the mines or the old times in their native Europe. When I was traveling nearby I would pitch in, as would my brother-in-law.

We put a slab of plywood between three trees supported with two-by-fours. Then we coiled a hose on the plywood. The water would be heated by the sun in summer for our showers. In cooler weather we would build a wood fire in an oil drum and heat cans of beer.

Whenever traveling nearby, I would always take Mom out, first to the local Sallies (Salvation Army) used clothing store. When she came out of the store I would often say:

"Mom you look bulkier now then when you went in."

"Never mind that. Just pay attention to the road."

Then lunch at the Boston Tea shop (where the right people lunched) and afterward to the dairy for honey dew ice cream.

Mom never acknowledged the money I had sent home. Nor did she ever comment on how much she enjoyed being out of the janitor basement apartment or being surrounded by trees and a lake and being free of janitor chores. (Years later when I finally did ask about the money she snapped: "I never saw a penny of it. If you sent it to your father he spent it all on beer and tobacco.") I never saw beer or alcohol in the house.

No matter. Mom finally got the house in the country (but no white picket fence) where she could watch the world go by as the song goes:

... and watch the rest of the world go by."

ON THE ROAD AGAIN

We left Odessa in the Texas panhandle for Taos, New Mexico, on Route 66. Tumbleweed, the ever receding horizon, rolling dark clouds, The night sky closed in on us; no other cars, alone on a lunar landscape. I drove all night. When my eyes started to close I would open the window and stick my head out into the cold spring desert air.

Ivan Michael Koenigsburg had been to Taos before selling pictures, knocking on doors, he would make an appointment for an interested housewife with a photographer who would at a later date show up with a pony so the kids could have a photo on a donkey. Michael talked about his evenings on the plaza dancing with the Taos Latinas.

The crew was still asleep when we pulled into Taos. But there was a problem. No cash. Michael did not get enough of our cash from Vic Moskowitz, the boss who owned RS, this mobile bookstore, the boss and mobile banker who safe guarded our savings (aka "good side").

So as soon we had a some breakfast I grabbed with my sales kit, hit doors and got enough deposits in 4 hours for lunch and dinner.

* * *

We all did well in Taos and put aside some more good side (cash savings). Coincidentally there was to be a festival in town that would consume a three day weekend and occupy all the public spaces. So with some extra cash and free time, Sammy Granzski, always with ideas came up with a plan.

"We should go to Jaurez, Mexico. Izzy, too, ain't it Izzy?"

We arrived in El Paso late afternoon where we left the car and walked across the border into Mexico. We wandered the streets looking for postal cards to mail home to prove we were in a foreign country. We noticed we were being followed by a cab that sported a sign: CHARLIE #1 TAKE YOU WHERE YOU WANT TO GO ENGRISH SPANICH CHINESE. Finally the driver opened his window.

"Charlie Number One Take You Where You Want to Go. Talk engrish? Spanish? Wha you wann. Food, Ladies. Take you where you wanna go."

"Steak and beer,"

We were not old enough to drink in the US and steak was cheap in Mexico.

"Take you America cafe."

None of us had much experience with beer. I knew enough to stop after one but they were insisting that we could have more. I was getting worried about them.

"Les go wid Charlie Chinese where you wanna go, Ha Ha."

Finally, "No more beer. Let's go."

Charlie was waiting at the curb. Maybe we were the only gringos in town.

"Take you where you want to go."

Charlie took Sammy and Izzy to a bar and then took me back into El Paso to my car where I fell asleep.

Somewhere in the middle of the night a knock on the window. Charlie.

"They want more money. Mas dinero amigo. Gèng du? qián."

I wasn't going to give Charlie some of their "good side" so I had him drive me back to the bar where he had left them. It was really late. Time to head back to Taos. I asked him to wait, I went through the swinging saloon doors when Sammy with a snout full of beer came through the door holding a young Latina by the waist. "thish Jaunita. marry and take her back home ..... live with Ma and Unca Henry."

I said that was a great idea and we could come back tomorrow to make the necessary arrangements. Charlie drove us back to El Paso and we drove the moonlit roads back to Taos.

We cycled back East again and in Cincinnati we hired a pretty, bright 18-year-old for my crew. She turned out to be a good producer. Rose and I got along well, visited each other's families and soon were married. About that time we had been working around West Chester and decided that we had had enough of hotels and restaurants We rented a flat over a barn in the country at Lake Mahopac in West Chester County, New York, not far from Scranton. I was hitting doors in nearby Bridgeport, Connecticut.

One Sunday visiting in nearby Scranton I was driving with a high school friend when I saw a Mercedes in front of Dolbitsky's house. My friend said it belonged to Joe Doran. Joe, like me, was in some kind of direct door-to-door sales. He worked for a guy named Mello. I knew of the Mello family since one of their kids who was retarded would often drop into our basement apartment where Mom would give him a cup of tea.

2: HITTING DOORS IN EUROPE

called Link Mello.

"Be on the *Liberte* (a WWI war German luxury liner given to France as reparations), Pier 42, February 8. I'll pay fare for you and the wife. You'll pay me back out of commissions." We'll be stopping in Paris on our way to Germany where you'll be selling to the GI's in Frankfurt."

At seat assignment on the *Liberte* we were asked if we would mind sitting with a negro. (This was 1956.) That night at dinner we were sitting with a tall slender black man from Mississippi who played blues alto sax in Paris: Big Bill Brounzie. Although we were in 3rd Class we had access to 1st class but the people were stuffy so we stayed with Big Bill.

In Paris we walked the streets fascinated by the houses, buildings, subway, the museums and always on the lookout for a hamburger joint. And we found one by window shopping: Pam Pam on the the Champs Elyses.

Then Link called telling us to meet him at the train station. When we arrived he was peeling out American bills to the conductor who escorted us to a cabin complete with a toilet and a double bed. The train was the Orient Express. The conductor seeing how green we were told us it went across Europe all the way to Russia.

The next morning we awoke to a winter wonderland in Augsburg. The snow must have been four feet deep. There were ice sculptures in the square. A magic world. Checked in at the Augsburger, we met our fellow door knockers: Henri Znati from France and Lenny Pole from England.

At dinner that night we learned that Henri was well educated, spoke excellent English, came from a moneyed background. His story was that he had married a ballet dancer but never consummated the marriage, His family disowned him for it but he supported her financially which is why he was here selling Encyclopedias. Who knows?

Lenny had the heavy cockney accent common in the Cheapside neighborhood of London. He liked to say to customers "Ask the man who owns one."

We did well in Augsburg. I was surprised how easy sales were: All the non-commissioned officers, staff sergeants, warrant officers, lived in apartments arranged in rows. So all the units were close together, and most importantly each door had the name and rank of the occupant written on the door. I would knock and when asked "who is there?"

"Hey Sarge it's Richie from Scranton." Almost always they would open and seeing a 22-year-old cleancut American civilian they would invite me in. First of all they seldom saw a US civilian, especially a 22-year-old. Secondly there was little diversion in Germany at this stage of rebuilding and there were no English language movies or TV. And they were bored with military talk from the Stars and Stripes media.

Also they realized they needed more education even if they stayed in the military. And the wife was almost always a German or French who was struggling with English and was eager for education.

The monthly payments were low. There was little to spend money on since consumer goods were rare. For example the major department store did not carry readymade women's maternity dresses but did sell material for those who could sew or find a seamstress. So why not buy an encyclopedia?

We had canvassed all the GI housing and it was time to move on. At this point Link showed up with a brand new Mark 7 Jaguar he had just picked up in Paris. He handed us the keys as he left for Italy and we drove the snowy mountain roads to Schwisch Gmund (close to Berchtesgaden, the site of Hitler's Eagles Nest). Again life-sized ice sculptures.

We checked in to the Gmund Hof on the second and third floors above a bakery. Much of the lobby was taken up by a billiard (as opposed to a pool) table. In the morning Frau Schultz would serve us coffee; better than I had ever had. I was told it was from Mexico which exported its best coffee. (Try coffee in an American taqueria!) With that soft boiled eggs and buttered rolls baked downstairs. Lunch was oxtail soup rich with the fat from the oxtail, fat we needed to combat the severe cold. Then much time on the billiard table. In the evening either before or after dinner we knocked on doors. We had covered all the houses in two profitable weeks and Henri drove us to the train in Stuttgart which took us to Frankfurt to canvass the many US non-coms lodged in GI housing.

Charlie Hyott from South Carolina met us at the station.

"I have a furnished apartment waiting for y'all close by, $125 US a month. All utilities paid."

Frau Limer met us at the door.

"Schonen tag."

She then, with list in hand walked us through the inventory of items including pot-hooks in the cupboard, towel racks, light bulbs, light switches, toilet paper holders, faucets; everything down to the smallest item. We signed the list and moved in with our suitcases.

Again it was very cold. We watched the people bundled up in heavy coats carrying briefcases which in fact carried lunch. Cheeks red from the cold.

The cars parked on Koerner Strasse in front of our house made for a pre-war antique car show. There were Citroens with the sweeping running boards and the inflatable springs, the model De Gaulle used. There was a 1939 BMW coupe convertible, a diesel pre-war Mercedes, the three-wheel Messerschmidt where the entry door was a see-through cockpit type top which one lifted up and stepped into one leg at a time, the 3-wheel Isetta Bubble car which one entered by swinging the front wall of the car open and then backing in. Best of all there was the S-Bahn (trolley car) around the corner looking like our San Francisco cable car with open sides and a running board to hang on. This took me to the GI housing.

We had picked up enough street German to shop, direct the cab driver and order food at the restaurant. At the butcher shop I would always give the Heil Hitler salute, never thinking of how touchy that could be. The butcher just laughed. Crazy Americanish.

HERR JUELGE TEACHES FLYING

The English language periodical was the European edition of the *NY Herald Tribune* where I found an ad offering flying lessons. Having free time during the day I took the train to Darmstadt, a village not far from Frankfurt. At the Darmstadt station there was a woman with a coffee cart who directed me to a dirt road that took me to the *flugplatz* (the landing strip): a large sheep barn complete with sheep and a man calling himself Herr Juelge, a captured Luftwaffe pilot who the Russians had doing test flights of Russian planes until war's end. He and Herr Rot were rhe flight instructors and in fact the entire business. In the barn there was a Piper Cub—their only asset. My understanding was that the WWII treaty forbade the Germans to own aircraft. This one had come in a crate from NYC, kit to assemble.

Neither Herr Julge or Herr Rot spoke more than a few words of English.I had by now a smattering of German.

Wie viel kosten die Kurse? (How much the classes?)

Kurse kostet USD $ 30 pro stunde. (Classes cost US $30 per hour.)

So between my broken German and their broken English we made it work.

Lesson 1 consisted of a tour of the instruments and then a live demo with Herr Julge at the controls. However this was still a sheep field and as lessons progressed we often had to stop to wait for the sheep to clear the field.

Wir müssen auf die Schafe warten. (We have to wait for the sheep.)

I liked it. From the International Business School (coincidentally in Scranton where my Mother had worked) I got a book on flying and the Bernoulli Theory which explains how planes fly.

Finally Herr Julge indicated I was ready for my solo flight. I circled the field twice and then was about to land. But I was approaching the field much too high. Instead of a final approach of say 8 feet I was coming in at about 20 feet. The idea was to stall (stop flying and and be pulled to earth by gravity). Stalling at 20 feet (dropping 20 feet) might have wrecked the plane, their only plane. Herr Julge was below wildly waving me off. Somehow I got the message and accelerated out of the slowdown and on the next try came in for a stall at about 6 feet.

ZIEGFRIED TEACHES ME ENGLISH

The flying and reading the Bernoulli theory got me thinking that maybe I should use my free time learning something else since there was no payoff for me in flying. So I contacted Frankfurt University asking for a tutor to teach me German. A young man, about 5 years younger than me, very blond, square jawed, sparkling blue eyes, showed up and we talked for a while. His father had been killed on the Russian front which entitled him to free University education. His immediate goal was to get 12 Marks (about $3) for a new tire for his bicycle.

We talked for a while then he asked some questions about grammar in very good English.

"What is the past participle of the verb to be?"

"Past what."

"Ok. Can you conjugate the verb to be?"

"Wait, hold on. Con, conju. What's that?"

After a few more questions:

"I can't teach you German. You don't know English. First I teach you English."

At the time I didn't know what that meant but since he was at University I was willing to listen. Later in sessions with him, I began to understand what he meant by English grammar. I didn't know the parts of speech, sentence structure, verb forms, past tenses, future tense, etc. But to him this was essential. So while I worked on this he also had me reading novels. Some easy ones then Tolstoy's *War and Peace.* I bought a dictionary and looked up maybe an average of 10 words per page. I was surprised to find that I liked reading and language lessons. Rose also read the books and we had fun talking about the characters like Mrs Marmaladov in *Crime and Punishment.*

Meanwhile I was making and saving money. We traveled to Rome where I had my first cup of real coffee—espresso.

The rental car guy:

"Paisano I buy you coffee."

A huge machine oozed tiny drops of thick black fluid. I was hooked.

Then Rose announced she was pregnant. We went to the local hospital. It was dark, spare, a victim of the war. The Doctor was huge with thick hands and of course spoke very little English with his booming voice.

"No good. I need to go back to the States to have my baby."

I had come to love life in Germany where money was plentiful. Things were cheap if you had dollars; All was clean and orderly. I had found a new me as I read and learned. And I had become an altar boy in the local Church attended by the GIs. I had found a home.

I was close tears about leaving but back we had to go. My goal now was college. I was hooked on books. This was to guide all my decisions about work and where we would live.

On the return we stopped in London and Dublin. In London we stayed at a Hotel across from the Marble Arch. Then we took a bus ride. But we went round and round but never heard the bus driver announce the Marble Arch.

"Do you go past the Marble Arch?"

"You mean Mablatch?"

After Dublin we flew in a 4-engine propeller plane to Gander, Labrador for refueling. Then New York and a ride back to Scranton.

I was advised by Link that I should work Fort Dix, New Jersey, where there was a lot of GI housing. There I ran into another door-to-door salesman who told me about selling Mutual Funds to the GIs.

"You can group pitch instead of one person at time."

BACK TO SCHOOL: This Time Like I Mean It

Meanwhile I tried to enroll in Rutgers College, NJ.

"Your grades are not acceptable. Try going to evening college where you can establish some grades."

I enrolled in night school at Ryder College.

Six months later I had some grades but Rutgers would not overlook my high school record.

"I can not ask the admission staff to look at these grades."

Then I tried King's College (College of Christ the King) in Wilkes-Barre. The admissions counsellor was a priest so I went heavy on my Catholicism, my altar boy experience in Germany, my coal miner background, my wife and new baby.

"Father I have no money but I work at night and can pay monthly."

I was in.

3: HITTING DOORS IN BERKELEY

We had rented a house just outside of Wilkes-Barre. Although I had saved about $5000 from Germany I realized that we would soon have a baby and that the money would go fast so I was out selling every night usually in the boonies. Sure enough the money was going fast. So approaching the end of the school year, having gotten good grades in economics and French, etc., I began to think that I needed to move out of the Valley. The Valley people did not have enough household income to support a lot of sales. The place that I remembered from my days with Reader's Service as being prosperous with good weather was Berkeley, California. So in the school library I looked through the catalog of colleges in the Bay Area and found one: University of California. I had never heard of it But I had good memories of the area. By now I could write a legible letter so I wrote for an application with a cover letter about my work and travel in the US, work in Germany, my grades at King's College, my origins in a coal miner culture.

They replied. UC Berkeley had a program for people who were older, traveled and had not had an opportunity to attend college right out of high school. That was me. I was accepted. Now the trick was to get there.

I drove Rose and the baby to Russell Springs, a small town in Kentucky where her dad had a small farm. We spent some time there picking tobacco on his small tobacco farm allotment and then went to Cincinnati where most of her brothers and sisters lived since there was no work in Russell Springs. The plan was to conserve as much cash as possible, so we agreed that she and the baby would stay with sister Rachel in Cincinnati, I would hook up with someone driving to California, once there get some cash by knocking on doors, rent a suitable place and then send her a plane ticket; all this while I adjusted to UC Berkeley. Naive?

I found a guy in the newspaper that was looking for a passenger to share gas. A Croatian from Zagreb, driving a Hudson. He never let me drive so we had to stop when he got tired losing time. We slept in the car except for one night in a YMCA. His English was not good and he may have been hard of hearing so we didn't talk and there was no radio. By the time we had reached barren eastern Nevada I was regretting the arrangement when a car pulled ahead of us and waved us down. I walked up to the car and spoke with the young woman who said she was headed to Fort Ord to meet up with her husband and wasn't sure of the way, was very tired of driving. I asked if she wanted me to drive.

I went back to the Hudson grabbed my bag returned to her car and got into the drivers seat. I stayed at the wheel till we got to Berkeley, checked into the Y.

I had $5 in my wallet. I got out my sales kit and started hitting doors. In two hours I had enough for some dinner and for breakfast the next morning. Next I needed to get money for books, a place for my wife and son, some basic furniture and plane tickets for them. Once I could locate where my classes would be I could get on with that other stuff.

I headed from the Berkeley Y to Dwinelle Hall through the Eucalyptus Grove. Green grass, Eucalyptus, handsome buildings and all these healthy beautiful young people lounging in the sun. Uh? I mean shouldn't they be studying or working? Looking at these young students lounging at Dwinelle Hall I felt more confident. They didn't know a Stillson wrench from a Phillips screw driver. I had six years of work experience and traveled all over the US and Europe. As a kid I had shoveled coal, shoveled snow, put show chains on tires in freezing weather, was a blacksmith apprentice, manned a boiler, was a janitor in an apartment house, scrubbed floors, washed windows.

And I was proud of my work feeling lucky that I had learned so many skills as a kid.

So now looking at these beautiful people loafing in the sun I thought, if they can do it, I can do it.

Little did I know.

I had never talked with anyone who took studies seriously so I had no idea how much work went into building a background that would support serious school work. I had come with the idea that I would take engineering since my people were all fixers, miners working with all the tools and equipment in the coal mines, men who nurse a few more miles out of exhausted Fords, building rustic homes for their families, hustling extra money as neighborhood handy-men, blacksmithing, welding. So I tried to enroll in engineering classes.

But this place was all about math, First thing was to take the math test. I did so badly that I was told that I would have to take the bonehead math course. Then I was doing poorly in bonehead math. I had no math background, only elementary algebra. I was told I would need calculus which required trig which required geometry which required advanced algebra etc. But I was already 23 and had a wife and child waiting for me back East. I didn't have time for all that.

In addition, for the first six weeks I did not have the math or chemistry books. What money I did have went into housing and the plane ticket for Rose and Mark. Soon I would be looking at failing grades and maybe suspension.

So here in the land of opportunity, why didn't I have those math skills? No matter, I needed to find a workaround.

I was doing ok with French and History and one of the French teaching assistants was from my Valley back home. Hearing my Valley accent he asked how I was adapting to California and UC. He heard my story and offered to help me. So I switched to French and History, and I was actually enjoying classes and doing well.

No worry about employment with a degree in French and History. In the fifties if you could write your name you could find a job.

On my first day in history class the TA, Marvin asked the class, "why are you here?" Never short on words I answered:

"I want to know why my father worked in the coal mines, my mother cleaned houses and why we lived in the janitor's basement apartment when everyone else in the area lived in lovely homes above ground, owned cars and didn't do dirty work."

He said, "I will answer that question."

I had found a home.

One day after class the French professor—an Algerian—called me aside:

"Are you from Texas? All I ever see you wear are jeans and boots."

"Not Texas. Pennsylvania. These are my only pants and the boots are army surplus."

"Ok. I am cleaning out my closet and have some clothes that might fit you."

I couldn't picture that since he was maybe 38 or 40 waist and I was a 30, even after a good meal.

Of course I accepted and eventually handed the clothes out to neighbors.

Meanwhile I was selling each evening and that was going ok. In six weeks I had enough money to send Rose a plane ticket, rent a bungalow on Walnut Street for $125/month about a mile from campus, purchase two sofa beds and a second-hand frig. Also for $35 I bought an oak table and chairs and I was able to rent a car to pick Rose and Mark up at the airport and pick up the crib Dad had sent RR Express. And I was able to buy the books (six weeks after class had started). All cash. Credit cards were not part of our culture.

With the switch from engineering there was less pressure, better grades and time with Rose and the baby. On Sunday instead of work, we walked up to Telegraph Ave with Mark sitting in the stroller for an espresso or an ice cream. And we got clothes or kitchen utensils at the Salvation Army.

One Sunday with some extra cash we took the train to San Francisco, then took the street car to the Zoo (free back then) and on the way back stopped at Tad's steak house for a steak and baked potato for $1.89 each. Luxury.

At home we ate a lot of swordfish which was about the cheapest protein in the Shattuck Avenue Coop Market. One neighbor had an orange tree, another had a fig tree. Not so bad. On our block there were a number of couples—some with kids—where one or both were working students. The wife in one of the families—from Israel—invited four neighbor women for tea but only used one tea bag. Hot water can be refreshing.

I didn't like door-to-door sales but I was good at it. It was the quickest, easiest way to make the money we needed for our very modest life style. And there was no boss, I was the boss. No forms to fill out. No bureaucracy. Just grab my sales kit, hold my nose knowing it would be all over in a few hours and hit a door. Make the sale or not, there was always another door to hit. When I made a sale I got the down payment, mailed the contract to Vic Moskowitz, the boss. He mailed me a check.

I always left home with only enough cash for a one way bus ticket: an incentive to make sure I got sales. But .... One night I was in the Fillmore which was all usually good territory on paydays. But this Friday evening I had gotten only checks. No cash for the bus back to Berkeley. So as the evening wore on I was getting desperate. So late in the evening I finally got another customer but again checks. She had no cash. I said, "wait are those soda bottles over there on the porch?" I took enough soda bottles to make up a deposit, cashed them at the corner grocery store and caught the bus home.

UNLOADING SHIPS: THE SAN FRANCISCO WATERFRONT

One Christmas vacation period I was told by my neighbor about a temporary opening on the waterfront doing longshore work. A break for me from hitting doors. The story was that the regular longshore guys would call in sick during the holidays. It paid $37 for an eight-hour night shift, big money. Back in the days before there were containers there was a lot of manual labor unloading ships, getting cargo out of the hold at the lower levels of the ship.

One of the guys who was in the same financial bind as me was going home for the summer and had left me in charge of his Vespa scooter so I had that for transportation to the San Francisco waterfront for the longshore job. Good but when it rained I got wet and stayed wet a good part of the night. And I was chewed out the first night on the job for wearing flip flops.

During the lunch break I would climb the gangplank and ask to see the ship. The ships from France were immaculate, all the seamen wore a u, even if it was just a T shirt and navy jeans. And they were usually happy to let me look around.

"Allez- y." (Go for it.")

Once in a while a box of liqueur would fall and break as it came out of the hold. This would be covered by insurance, so not wanting to put a broken box with broken bottles on a delivery truck the longshoremen would tidy it up. One crew down in the hold of the ship loading cargo on palettes to be hoisted on deck was sent home early and their pay was docked. They did more with the booze than clean up the broken bottles.

The Produce Market was just across from the Ferry Building where the Embarcadero Center now stands. When our shift was over at 4am I walked with the regulars through the Produce Market, lit up by flames dancing in empty oil drums fed by pieces of produce crates. It bustled with farmers and restaurant people buying fresh produce for the day. I followed the crowd to Fisherman's Wharf for breakfast. Nearby was a tent city, a large building, once a warehouse —now an expensive motel—divided into rooms with blankets hanging from the ceiling; one tenant was a friend who taught history at the Art Institute.

Christmas holidays over, the longshore guys were back and I was hitting doors again.

JACK

One evening late on the way home from the library I stopped to look at some magazines at the cigar store on Telegraph. I was on average 6 years older than most of the students and, dressed in army surplus clothes, I did not look like a student. A guy started talking to me and eventually asked me about work opportunities. He was a student and needed money. Perfect. A clean looking guy, obviously not shy about talking to strangers, bright and needy. To knock on doors we need to be needy. I explained the deal to him. I would welcome someone to talk with about work and on the bus to and from work and I would be getting a commission on sales that he made. With or without the commissions I needed someone to talk to. The solitude only made hitting doors worse.

As I got to know Jack I saw him as someone who had been seduced by the media version of college life. He had been a good student, he looked good and he had a car. But none of this was sustainable. The car was falling apart. Jack had no money to maintain it or even to support himself. Getting good grades was difficult without enough food, or books or toothpaste. His family had no money. He did have a girlfriend on campus (essential for the media image) but she tired of never having an occasional hamburg at Kips the campus burger joint, and moved on. His background unfolded as we talked on the bus going out to territory (the neighborhood where we hit doors). His real father John Leckage Lamar was a handsome 50-year-old teenager. Never quite up to sharing himself with a family. His stepfather was Woody; we called him "Forever Woody" since he was totally devoted to Jack's mother Honey, no matter what. Woody had been a navigator on a bomber in WWII and retired on a pension too small to provide for himself and Honey. To make ends meet after retirement from the Air Force he always found a job managing a motel where the job would include a free one-bedroom apartment. Not just any motel but the kind that are smack on the freeway usually behind a sound barrier wall, where you might see old model dilapidated cars parked, where you might wonder why the sheets smelled the same as the perfume on the woman just checking out. In one such motel just south of the SFO airport in the unincorporated area of the county, behind a sound barrier wall, he was signing out a guy who pulled a gun and cleaned out the register. The second time it happened, Woody left. Eventually Woody got the super's job at a subsidized senior resident building.

Honey was Jack's mother. In her younger days she had been a model in Arkansas when she met and married Lamar. Shortly thereafter Jack was born, Honey doubled her weight, Lamar left. Enter Forever Woody. Now eighteen years later Honey was three times her model size but still had the blond hair. In spite of her bulk she still struck a model's pose, holding a cigarette as she covered her mouth to smother the ever persistent cough. I recall watching her opening the frig just wide enough to slide behind the door while still talking to me.

"It's so nice to meet ya'll finally."

"She does that frig door routine so she can sip cold vodka all day." Devastating as Honey was to Jack's imagined self image, she was his mother; he tried to be respectful.

At last Honey was bedridden. Woody was still the totally forever attendant.

Honey still had her Arkansas drawl so when she called Woody there was an emphasis the the DY as in Woody, WooDY, WOODY!

Jack was a natural. He memorized the spiel in no time, watched me for an hour and then set out in the opposite direction on the block. This was a Filipino area just behind the SF Post Office. When I got around the block on Natoma Street, a door opened and there was Jack with a bowl of Adobo. He had made his first sale and had made sniffing gestures, saying Masarap (smells good). We worked that area clean for the sales were easy and there was always the vinegar, soy sauce odor of Adobo and the sweetest people.

LOADING BOX CARS

That summer Jack went home. I got work at Railway Express in the Refer (Refrigerator car) loading Bok Choi (a Chinese cabbage) just in from the farms in the Valley. Each box addressed to an Asian restaurant in a different town on the main railroad line from Oakland to Portland, Maine. I wondered what life must have been for the kids of those Chinese families living in small towns across America where there were no other Asians. I did ask a Chinese woman what it was like for her three daughters growing up in South Bend where her husband taught math at Notre Dame. She said there were lots of Chinese for social life in nearby Chicago. (Nearby?) Later I find her three daughters married whites.

The other guy working the Refer with me was an older man who was an expert on railroad history which is essentially the post-Civil War history of America. Very pleasant and fun to talk with I finally got the nerve up to ask him how he could marry his love of history with this manual, boring labor. He explained something I would come to know only too well in later life. He said he was philosophical about it. There was no money for college, he married young and had a retarded child which made a steady paycheck first priority, so he struck it out loading Bok Choi at RR Express. Another unsung hero.

Sometimes the guys in the next Refer would be loading Manilla or Cherry Stone Clams. And as luck would have it sometimes a container would fall and break spilling the clams all over the platform. Common decency kept us from loading them into a truck. Imagine a restaurant in Kokomo, Indiana getting a half empty container of clams and how that would reflect on the RR Express. So we all had clams for dinner the next day.

By now Mark was a vocal 2-year-old so on Sunday—day of no work—he would ride on my back in a hike-a-poose up to Telegraph for an ice cream for him and an expresso for Rose or if the weather was cold there was firewood stored under the pedestrian bridge at nearby Live Oak Park. I would get a few logs and Mark and I would sit in front of the fire. At Christmas we would wait until Christmas morning when the tree lot next to the Shattuck Avenue Coop would be deserted with the Christmas trees lying free on the ground. And there were the used clothing and furniture stores down on Adeline. On weekends Rose would roll up all the laundry in a bed sheet for me to haul to the washer house a few blocks down Vine Street. Good study time.

UC administration wrote me that there was something for me to pick up at the UC office. It was an anonymous gift of $100. Wow. My guess it was from a history professor whose father—he told me in an Office Hours session—had been a manual laborer like mine.

School started again. Jack returned and we were back hitting doors. But Jack had gotten spoiled with vacation and Honey waiting on him at home so he started whining.

"Let's find something else to do for money. No more banging on doors in the cold."

"Ok I get it. This is tough but it works. My idea is if it works don't fix it. Besides time looking for another kind of work and then adjusting to it is time away from studies and worse it means a temporary loss of money. My kids eat every day. Then I would walk him to the top of the Potrero Hill.

"Look east Jack. That's Harvard out there. You Jack are there in Graduate school. No more hitting doors when you get there because you are on a fellowship that pays all, including all you can eat. So let's get on with it and it will be soon graduation time. All you have to do is get through another night.

Normally we would get off the Berkeley to San Francisco bus at 2nd Street and go straight to the Jitney, 15 cents up to Mission and 24th, 25 cents beyond that but time permitting , we would first walk up to Foster's Cafeteria on Market. One us of would order a coffee—10 cents—and fill the emptied with half and half from the creme dispenser, Jack would drink it, then a coffee refill for 5 cents. That was part of Jack's dinner, the other part being the peanut butter and bread carried in his sales kit. (Later he would switch to caffeine pills—cheaper than coffee.)

THE CANNERY

Something popped up. Good money for swing shift. The cannery was hiring. We were hired along with our friend Antonio; because of our educational level we were put to measuring the lips on cans that had been rejected by the canning machine.

Our supervisor was a giant of a guy named Workman who carried a 2-foot long flashlight as if it were a police billy club and he wore a railroad engineer's cap. He was suspicious of students and especially of Antonio who was from Italy. There were only African Americans and Latino Americans in the cannery and Antonio did not fit either category. And Workman did not understand how measuring the cans fit into the cannery business. So any time he saw us talking or resting he would tell Antonio.

"I gonna send you back to Stromboli."

Once the can measuring was finished we were put on the production line to manage the canning machine. We were doing fruit cocktail. Peaches were done last month. The fruit—rock hard—was put into a can with a sugary syrup that would ripen it. Cans came down an assembly belt lined with women supposed to do a visual inspection of each can. But the cans were moving so fast I never did figure out how that worked. The destination of the the can was the actual canning machine which was circular with inverted pistons that would slam a top on a can and seal it as it moved from the entrance point of the circle to then it would exit the other side of the machine into another conveyor belt which would speed it—in seconds—to a machine that packed it into a box where another machine put it on a truck. This whole operation took only minutes. Our job was to knock the can off the machine if the inverted piston incorrectly placed the lid. We were given a stout stick the size of billy club. The cans moved at high speed and it was necessary to hit the can fast to avoid the piston hitting the stick or my hand. In one case a worker did not move fast enough and the piston cut his thumb off. It dropped into the can and in seconds was sealed with fruit cocktail and on the truck. It turned up for someone's breakfast in Seattle. My best memory of the cannery was hearing one of the assembly line women say "Maybellene I ain't seen y'all since the peaches."

After the fruit cocktail we were out of work and back to hitting doors. By now we were really burned out so to prime ourselves we would go into St. Francis Candy Kitchen on 24th St in the Mission—free refills—and drink coffee till our knees were in spasms, then back on the street. On Saturdays however we had a slightly different warm-up. Our sales kits were made of hard plastic so we would march down a sidewalk—there were always kids playing in the street—and banging on the sides of the sales kit with our hands we would march and whistle or sing John Phillips Sousa's *Stars and Stripes Forever* and the kids would follow us like the Pied Piper.

Occasionally on a Friday night or Saturday evening if we were close to North Beach we would go into clubs just to see—no bouncers or security guards back then—sit at an empty table until the waitress came by.

"Can I take your order?"

"Oh yeah, well we just came in to see what it was like."

"No problem. Stay until I need the table. But how about a glass of water? No charge."

CABBIE

Summer came, Jack went home to Riverside again and I took a job driving cab night shift. My territory was West Berkeley where most of the action was on San Pablo Ave. Young women provocatively dressed would cab from bar to bar sometimes with a client. It was depressing. I couldn't just say well that's the way it is.

One night I was driving a guy who was just about to get out when I heard a metallic click in the back seat and the voice said something like you M....... F.......

I gonna kill you." That was enough for me. I quit and went back to hitting doors.

Occasionally on the way to work from class I would go into Harmon Gym and watch the gymnasts doing giant swings on the high bar, doing handstands on the rings or going hand over hand up the rope. Eventually I would be able to do some of that myself just from watching. The coach Lou Perske would see me and—realizing that I had no training and could not afford the time to take the class—would come by with some pointers.

In the four years that I spent at UC Berkeley I never attended an event on campus but these furtive ten-minute sessions at Harmon Gym gave me the feeling I belonged.

Eventually being out nights, hitting doors in the rain and not enough sleep I got sick and the Doc at the campus medical clinic determined that I had strep throat and assigned me to a bed in the clinic. Paradise. No hitting doors, no class, three meals a day, TV. But it only lasted 3 days and anyhow Rose was almost out of money so back to hitting doors.

One evening in the jitney heading into the Mission, Jack introduced me to a classmate. Bill Issel was a native San Franciscan and like me had kids and of necessity worked nights to support his family. We became friends. Once he loaned me his history class notes. I read them and when he asked for them back I explained that I had thrown them away. When he seemed surprised I explained that the class was over so why the concern.

At that point I realized that my attitude toward the UC experience needed to change. Up to then I had the idea that the entire process was a ritual for mostly rich legacy kids. But here was a guy like me sweating it out with little money, working nights and taking this process seriously. It woke me up: gave me respect for the process and Bill became my model. My performance improved and my resolve strengthened.

Later Bill and I wanted to do a course in French History but the book was expensive so we split the book with me reading one week and him reading it the next.

DOGPATCH

In what is now known as Dogpatch, on a windy cold Saturday afternoon I was working the blocks alone. It was late but I decided to hit one more door. It was a small stand-alone house, a kitchen chair and a frig on the narrow front porch. A large pleasant looking women opened the door emitting an odor of something from the oven that must have added a glow to my eyes. She invited me in. At the kitchen sat a small thin man and a a middle aged Down's Syndrome woman. They were speaking Italian. As I went through the spiel they showed no interest, but just as when I getting ready to leave the woman was taking from the oven a loaf of bread and a Frittata. I sniffed and muttered "oh." She smiled and asked if I would like some and when I was seated she poured me a glass of red. How do I thank people I will never see again. Guys from Scranton don't cry.

CHINATOWN

I heard about a part time evening job at the California State Health Department which had an office within walking distance. The woman in charge, a kindly motherly type explained that it was a survey on health and alcohol use. And the slot to be filled was San Francisco's Chinatown. She asked if I would be comfortable knocking on doors in Chinatown. Knocking on doors? I knew something about hitting doors, Latinos in the Mission, Polish in Detroit, Irish in Boston, African Americans in the SF Western Addition, Italian and Hasidim in Brooklyn, but so far no Chinese. So why not?

As a kid in Scranton the Saturday matinee at the local Bell theatre would show a short between the main film and the cowboy movie. One of the series was Fu Man Chu the inscrutable, with the pigtail, gown, the cap. Another series showed Detective Charlie Chan with a white detective side kick. Charlie Chan said very little—which fit the image we had of inscrutable Chinese. This only added gravity to the few brilliant words he muttered as he examined evidence. None of these Chinese screen characters were played by Asians. They were played by white guys who mimicked what they thought were Chinese accents. What did we know?

The State Health Department woman in charge was happy to hear about my door-to-door experience as she showed me the question form, the list of acceptable answers and the possible excuses. One of them: "No English." And the list of the preselected addresses in Chinatown. Monday mornings I would show up with the results.

So first evening out I hit a door in Ross Alley. A middle age Chinese woman opened the door:

"No engrish."

"No problem. We're doing a survey for..."

"No engrish"

From the next room came a voice;

"Ma who is it."

"A salesman."

"Tell him no english"

"No english. What you selling anyway."

"Ma we don't want any. No english."

The door slammed shut.

Better luck next door.

"How many alcoholic drinks do you drink per day?"

"No drink."

"Does this interfere with your normal routine?"

"No drink."

I was surprised at how many people cooperated. But I did get a lot of "No English."

THE CHEN FAMILY

One address was on an alley. The sign said "Men Only Hotel." I rang and an elderly man answered. He spoke English, name of Huang, and invited me to climb the steps with him to his room on the 2nd floor. There were quite a few mailboxes on the wall. On the way down the hall we passed what appeared to be a communal kitchen: sinks along one wall, each one alongside a gas ring stove and a cutting board. Men were cutting/chopping veggies and cooking in woks. Further down the hall we passed the communal bathroom. The residents' rooms occupied the east and west walls. Huang's room was about 10-by-10 with a single bed, a chair and a desk piled high with old Chinese newspapers. The window—covered at night by a yellowed paper shade—was open now to the sun. I sat in the only chair. Now I could get a better look at him as he sat on the bed. Small and lean, clean shaven, short white hair, a healthy ruddy complexion, clean pressed khakis and a blue work shirt. He pointed to a picture on the wall of two boys and a woman.

"Chen Family."

Recruited by a labor contractor from rural western China he boarded a ship and eventually arrived in San Francisco at 13-years-old where he was put to work washing dishes in the Street Cafe by the owner who was his immigration sponsor. Over the years he rotated through the cafe ranks and became a cook. A frugal life let him finally return to China to marry a young mail-order bride who soon became pregnant. He returned to San Francisco awaiting the news of the birth. Twin boys. He sent money for their upkeep and for photography. She sent pictures. He sent money. She sent pictures. He had a family. Now the boys were young adults The flight to China was too long now for Chen so instead he sent money for them to come. So far they had not come. But he had a family: The Chen Family. In Scranton boys don't cry.

PERE JACQUES VALENTE L'ECOLE POLYTECNIQUE

The French TA from my hometown in Pennsylvania, Mr. Kelly called me aside after class to say that a French priest—who was also a physicist—had recently arrived from the Sorbonne in Paris and was staying the St. Thomas rectory on campus and was looking for help in English. He added that it would be a good opportunity for me to improve my French. Mon., Wed., Fri. at 8am at the rectory which was on the northeast corner of campus.

In a cloud of cigarette smoke (French Gauloises, enough to scar the tonsils) mixed with the aroma of hi-octane espresso was Père Jean Valente, short, round, bald, penetrating blue eyes.

"Bonjour Monsieur John."

I mumbled "Bonjour." From there, we both struggled with me thinking that it would have been more productive for him to have a Francophone rather than me but for some reason he was ok with me. When he heard about my coal mine childhood and all the jobs I had held and the fact that I was a door-to-door salesman at night to support a wife and child he was happy and even happier that I was receptive to learning about an alternative economic system.

He explained right away that he was a Communist and saw that I showed no signs of being threatened. But to live he needed money and he got that by teaching physics at the University in France.

One Sunday the Père Valente came to visit with a physics grad student George who had 2CV Citroen (2 CheVaux which roughly translates to 2 horse-power).

They were fascinated by Rose's stories—which I always encouraged her to tell—about being raised on a small truck/tobacco farm in Russell County, rural Kentucky where playing the horses was the sport.

"Why Uncle Red, he won $1000 last week but he lost it and some of his own this week."

She explained that her father had inherited land from his family and lost most of it on horses and dogs. The first day I visited there he—had in the trunk of his car—a dog he was about to trade for a farm tool.

To ensure some financial stability the women would go to work in Cincinnati, rent a room in boarding house and try to arrange a ride back to the "country" occasionally. When I first met Rose, her mother—a nurse's aide—was rooming in a neighborhood of Cincinnati called Camp Washington. Bathroom down the hall.

Hitting doors was going ok but then with Jack gone home again for break I got a job driving truck for the local Oakland newspaper delivering bundles of the *Tribune* to the suburbs. Driving to Walnut Creek or Lafayette I was struck by the fact that everyone there seemed to be either white or asian. Where were all the brown, black people we were accustomed to in Berkeley?

Jack returns. First The Candy Kitchen again to OD on caffeine then back on the street hitting doors.

VON KNEFFEL: BRACERO

Edmond Von Enfiel, a regular presence on Telegraph Ave was often at Cafe Med bent over what had been an espresso a few hours ago. From Hamburg Germany, his story was that his father was a pastor of a large Lutheran church in Hamburg and Edmond was here working on a bachelor degree. But Edmond was bald, with a paunch and a hesitant gait—most likely easily over thirty. Maybe even forty. Something wrong with his story? Edmond always like to talk about the days ahead after graduating.

"Top food, top women, top everything."

I gathered from something he said that his family stopped sending money, Soon after he went to an agricultural jobber in the valley and was hired as a field hand. I doubt that Edmond had ever worked in his life but now he was willing to try fieldwork picking fruit or vegetables in the blazing sun; back-breaking work even for those who had done it all their lives. Also it seemed he only owned suits. I didn't see him when he left for the valley but he probably wore a suit and a vest.

He told us that at the end of the first work day he didn't eat but just fell asleep on the army cot in the tent in the stifling valley heat. The next morning he could not get out of bed. Finally in the afternoon he did and hitched a ride back to Berkeley. I could picture him, overweight in a European dress suit, including a vest bent over, picking crops in the merciless heat alongside the braceros. No top food, top women, no top anything. But he tried.

By now our son Mark was an articulate 3-year-old. And Rose had given birth to a lovely girl we called Kelly. Soon we would have John, a fine baby boy. During our walks in the neighborhood we often passed a toy store on Oxford and Vine. In the window Mark spotted an Etch-a-Sketch, a toy that allows one to create lineographic images (drawings). Mark wanted it and explained how it worked and what he could do with it. But it was $3. So we put to on our wish list. With luck I would be graduating in a year and then ....

The County was holding an auction of used County property which I was told included vehicles, autos for as little as $50. Fifty bucks was a decent week's wage at the time. So I wrote to Vic, the Boss Moss asking for a loan. Then across Oakland by bus out to the Alameda equipment yard. I got a 52 Chevy two door—with front seat only—for $50. This gave us a lot more flexibility on where to sell and saved much time. Now we could work anywhere in SF, Oakland or the East Bay, and on Sundays we got to take the kids to the zoo (free at the time) and/or the park. The kids loved it and with no back seat it was easy to put the stroller in and Mark—tall enough to see over the front seat—could stand giving directions.

BOSTON

Boss Moss phoned about a new product. The idea was for Jack and I to go to Boston that summer to learn the new spiel. I got the feeling that he was happy with how well we were doing while we were at the same time going to school and so he wanted to make nice. He would front us the money to be paid back out of our sales. I made it clear that I wanted Rose and the kids to make the trip also so he got a place for a month at the Biltmore in Back Bay. My sister Dianne came up from nearby Scranton with Mom. Boss Moss loaned her his red Caddy convertible. and they toured historic Boston in style.

BAY OF PIGS INVASION CUBA

In April 1961 two months before I was to graduate a group of Cuban rebels who had fled Cuba when Castro took power devised with the covert aid of the

CIA to invade Cuba. The US was alarmed because Russia had ships close by and the fear was that the Cold War would become hot. A lot of students were very upset declaring no to war, saying this was risking the lives of low-income young men who were in the military since they had no better choices. A lot of students headed to Union Square to hear speeches denouncing the invasion including a speech by Sterling Hayden the star of the movie *Doctor Strangelove*. There was also a speech in Newman Hall by the head of the History Department, Dr. Sontag—who had been at the Nuremberg Trials—attempting to calm the students.

The CIA-financed invasion failed, some say because JFK refused to support it.

BRAVE NEW WORLD

Jack's professor in an advanced class got Jack, although still an undergraduate enrolled in a Graduate course. It was to be taught by a visiting professor Aldous Huxley. Huxley said in his 1932 book *BRAVE NEW WORLD* that the masses would be controlled through pleasure (bread and circuses) as opposed to George Orwell who said in his 1949 book entitled *NINETEEN EIGHTY FOUR* that the masses would be controlled by fear.

At the end of the course the students invited Huxley to a lunch to be given at one to the old large houses formerly owned by a professor but now a rooming house for students. Jack invited me. So there's Jack, a poor kid from a dust bowl family, and me, a coal miner's son, door-to-door book peddler having lunch with a world-renowned author. I don't remember what was said but I do remember the empty feeling of wanting to speak but having nothing to say. That was 1961.

Graduation was only a year away if all went well. After the hit my grade point had taken from chemistry and math in my first year I had managed to get enough A grades to get my average almost to B+. That was important since that would put me in the running for a fellowship in grad school which meant no more hitting doors. It meant more time learning, reading, associating with thinking people.

But I needed to get at least two more A's. I didn't like reducing learning to counting grades but I didn't like hitting doors either. There was a course in

Astronomy being given that summer by Helen Pilan. I needed one more science course. I went to talk to her before the course started and laid it out just as you see it here: my kids, hitting doors, the coal mines. All of it. Picture it. A twenty-seven-year old Irish kid, dressed in army surplus clothes from the coal fields of Scranton telling her I needed an A because I did not want to hit doors any more. And she listened. She really listened. We would sit at a table in the drugstore coffee shop at North Gate and she would answer my questions. I got the A. May whatever gods may be smile down on this woman.

In my last year I signed up for Ancient History. The course was fascinating but as I tried to weave it all together it kept falling apart. I had only gotten a B in the midterm. So I went to visit the Professor Bill Finnegan. I explained that I found it easier to recall events if could tie them together with a cause and effect narrative. He listened. He listened and he said he would give me what ever grade I got on the final.

Things were looking good. Rose had the house under control with the little money we had. The kids—two now with one more on the way—were fine. Everyone was healthy. But it was hard to concentrate, so many distractions: the soon to be Free Speech Movement was rumbling in the background, the Civil Rights movement, the sexual revolution, and feminism were gaining attention, the Cuban Missile Crisis, the hippies, beatniks, Jack Kerouac, Ferlinghetti, the Summer of Love in the Haight-Ashbury. And San Francisco had been discovered by students from all over the United States.

One warm Saturday after hitting the last door, I saw on the walk to the bus stop, a saloon. Thinking a cold beer but kept walking. Waiting for the bus the cold beer keep appearing in my mind's eye. Out of the question. All money was needed at home. The bus didn't come, did not come. My feet took me to that saloon. I heard a guy ordering a cheese sandwich on sourdough. Then I heard someone else ordering a cheese on sourdough except this someone else was me. I felt guilt as I ate it and will always remember how good it was.

GRADUATION

At last classes were over. Bill and I did not attend the Graduation Ceremony.

A few days later I got my grades in the mail. Yes, I got the A to give me a B+ average. We celebrated with fish and chips at Spenger's Fish House.

Jack? What happened to Jack?

The father of Jack's girlfriend Lenora, hoping to rid his daughter of this infatuation with what looked like a Berkeley hippie loser, floated her a ticket to Sweden—but Lenora took Jack with her to Sweden. After Lenora dumped him—having no money—he became a chalk sidewalk artist on the streets of Stockholm. It was at this point he coined his famous phrase:

"You can eat anything if you put enough soy sauce."

Earning very little money he got a subsidized apartment. He would later rent out the apartment to visitors and use the money to go to Bangkok.

On the day scheduled for return to Bangkok, as the cab to the airport waited, Jack threw the key though the transom. The janitor would let the renter in. But when Jack got to the cab he realized that he had left his passport. The janitor was not in. Jack tried to climb from the fire escape onto the balcony of the apartment. He fell. He died. The woman he was to marry in Bangkok got a lawyer suspecting foul play since a rich Swede had Jack in his will. But it all just faded away with time.

Ok, with a degree in hand I would never have to sell books again.

But wait. No. Not so fast.

We still needed rent and groceries. Until I found an alternative job with my new diploma I would have to hit doors. Oh no. Back on the street.

But a job at United Parcel Service came up. The hardest work I have ever done. It was in the Marina, all 2nd floor stuff, running up steps. For lunch one day I ate my sandwich at the Marina Library on Chestnut while I tried to read Hegel. I was so into it that I went through a stop sign at Chestnut and Sanchez. A car going north on Sanchez hit me, was diverted across the street, smashed into a building where it stopped. I was knocked out of the high seat in the truck onto the pavement; the truck hit a tree and stopped. I was not hurt. Neither was the other driver. I was fired. I never did figure Hegel out anyway.

A short while later I got an interview with a pharmaceutical company selling directly to stores. They loved my sales background. The rep drew me a diagram of the female anatomy and showed me how sanitary napkins worked. While he was doing the demo my brain was double thinking, was this why I spent four years at UCB?

But I didn't see any want ads asking for people to change the world either. Try to keep things in perspective! Meanwhile the job loading boxcars opened up again and I did that while scouring the want ads. Always do two things at once!

It turned out that one of the regulars at Mick Diller's house across the street was in the labor movement and set me up with an interview as a labor organizer with the Building Service Employees International Union (now the SEIU). Perfect. A decent income.

We bought Mark the Etch-a-Sketch. Then we ate our way through the Bay Area. No more oatmeal dinners.

A PAYCHECK

Just before I signed on as labor organizer I interviewed with the State of California. During the interview I noticed a guy about my age at a nearby desk watching and listening. On the bus going home that evening I happened to find myself sitting next to the guy, name of John Violet. We talked and he finally said that he was curious as to why I did not accept the job offer. Not wanting to downplay his job, I said I wanted to think it over. Frankly it did not sound exciting. Hitting doors—for all its problems—no paper work, no time clock and no boss: I had always been my own boss. We were walking in the same direction and—finding him congenial and his stories about his hometown New Orleans interesting, I invited him in for an espresso. Rose liked him and we arranged for him to come visit with his wife. We had new friends.

About a year after he came to me with a paper advertising fellowships for graduate school in City Planning. City Planning. What? Thanks but no thanks. I wanted grad school in history; he persisted and he was persuasive. Ok. I applied to City Planning Departments at five Universities. Oh my dog. I got five fellowship offers. Five!

But wait. One more try. A hail Mary pass.

I immediately went on campus to the Middle East Studies Deptartment and told the Arabic professor that I wanted to study Middle Eastern History. Anything to get back on the UC campus.

"No way. No Middle East language, no background."

Ok so now I had to look at these five offers. So I talked with the head of the History Department, a guy I could relate to, my campus hero. He asked "Which school offers the most money?" University of North Carolina, Chapel Hill offered me $4000/year.

"Then that's it."

But how to get there? The old Chevy no good. Then John Nicols—just finishing his Phd—took us to Ernie's for dinner to celebrate my fellowship. I told him about not having transportation. When we arrived home that evening he handed me the keys to his Ford. Problem solved. A '49 Ford 2 door.

We farmed out our meager furnishings with the promise I would return someday for my beloved round oak table. With baby John in the hike-a-poos strapped to the center of the back seat and Kelly and Mark on each side we set off across country. We had enough money saved for motels and restaurants which the kids thought was great. They especially liked the motel TV since we did not have one.

We ate our way across America.

And no more hitting doors.

Are you sure?

I promise.

Some people say they worked hard for what they have. But I say it's all luck and I thank the people and whatever gods may be who put luck in my way.

Thanks to:

Teddy Smulowitz, Vic Moskowitz, Tersh Boasberg, Dr. Sontag at UCB, Bill Freeling at UCB, Marc Rosen at UCB and Dr. Falk and Mr. Price at UNC, and the African American woman who kept insisting that I take the time to sit down and fill out the form to shift from temp to full-time Federal employee which entailed a pension. And to the author of Corporate Characters Wulf Reader *who encouraged me. Also to my parents who by example showed me perseverance. Thanks to Professor Bill Issel (author of* Coit Tower*) who was my inspiration and mentor.*